Get started Passive income retirement adaptability :

The key to financial independence. Turn your passion to profits

Bonus: Checklist for unlocking Financial freedom

James D. Lynn

All rights reserved. No part of this publication may be reproduced, distributed, or transmitted in any form or by any means, including photocopying, recording, or other electronic or mechanical methods, without the prior written permission of the publisher, except in the case of brief quotations embodied in critical reviews and certain other noncommercial uses permitted by copyright law.

Copyright © by James D. Lynn [January 2024]

Table of Contents

WHY SHOULD WE SCALE ON OUR INCOME IN THESE CHANGING TIMES?

Scaling income is critical in changing times for numerous reasons:

Inflation and Living Costs: During periods of transition, the cost of living may increase owing to inflation or economic developments. Scaling income allows you to keep your buying power while covering rising costs.

Uncertainty in the Job Market: Economic developments often cause job market swings. Income scaling diversifies your revenue sources, lowering reliance on a single source and offering financial security in the event of job loss or market turbulence.

Technological advancements: Rapid technology breakthroughs have the potential to provide new possibilities. Scaling income helps people to adapt to shifting trends, learn new skills, and explore new money streams.

Entrepreneurial chances: Changing times may bring new chances for entrepreneurs. Scaling income allows you to invest in business endeavors, startups, or side projects, allowing you to capitalize on chances for extra cash streams.

Globalization and Remote Work: As remote work and globalization become more prevalent, people may access a greater variety of revenue sources. Scaling income allows you to participate in global marketplaces and collaborate with a variety of customers or employers.

Retirement Planning: Traditional retirement models may change as economic environments change. Income scaling enables people to contribute more to retirement savings, guaranteeing financial stability and a decent retirement lifestyle.

Adaptability: Economic and cultural developments need flexibility. Scaling income emphasizes a proactive attitude to acquiring new skills, remaining marketable, and capitalizing on emerging trends.

Financial Resilience: Creating numerous revenue sources helps to build financial resilience. Having various income streams offers a cushion and lessens financial stress during times of economic uncertainty or personal hardship.

Scaling income increases progress toward financial objectives, whether they be housing, education, vacation, or early retirement. It enables people to attain their own goals and live a better life.

Long-Term Wealth Creation: Consistent income growth adds to long-term wealth creation. It enables smart investing, asset accumulation, and the establishment of a solid financial basis for future generations.

Scaling income in changing times is essentially a proactive technique that not only protects against uncertainties but also opens doors to new possibilities, allowing people to prosper and establish a financially resilient future

INTRODUCTION

SECTION I : THE KEY TO FINANCIAL INDEPENDENCE AND ECONOMIC FLEXIBILITY

Welcome to the route to financial freedom and economic flexibility, which holds the key to unlocking a future of autonomy and security. In a world defined by rapid change and shifting economic landscapes, the capacity to achieve financial independence has never been more important. This path is about more than just acquiring money; it is a systematic approach to obtaining control of your financial future and navigating the challenges of an ever-changing financial landscape.

As we go through the pages of this transformational journey, you will learn the skill of establishing sustainable passive income sources that are purposefully selected to line with your financial objectives. But this book is more than simply a handbook; it's a call to action, challenging you to proactively build your retirement with an aggressive mentality, seizing chances and bolstering your financial foundation.

Investigate the principles of passive income and investigate several paths such as real estate, stock market investments, entrepreneurship, and digital businesses. Discover the keys to producing not just money, but a robust financial plan suited to your own goals and circumstances. Beyond the confines of revenue creation, we'll delve into the complexities of retirement planning, discussing critical issues like lifestyle design, tax efficiency, and the ever-important balance of work and leisure. Join me in picturing a retirement that is not just safe but also dynamic—a stage of life marked by financial independence, personal satisfaction, and the ability to enjoy life on your terms.

So, whether you're a seasoned investor, an aspiring entrepreneur, or someone just starting their financial journey, "Get started Passive Income Retirement Flexibility" invites you to embark on a transformative quest—one that leads to financial abundance, aggressive retirement planning, and a future where your financial decisions pave the way for a life well-lived. Let the trip begin.

A new paradigm for retirement

Welcome to the dawn of a new paradigm for retirement—a departure from traditional notions of simply withdrawing from the workforce. In this evolving landscape, retirement is not merely an endpoint but a dynamic phase marked by financial empowerment, personal fulfillment, and the pursuit of passions.

Flexibility and Continued Engagement:

Retirement transcends a fixed age; it's about choosing when and how to step back from traditional work.

Emphasis on flexible work arrangements, part-time endeavors, or pursuing passion projects post-"retirement."

Financial Independence as a Journey, Not a Destination:

Shift from a singular focus on accumulating a lump sum for retirement to building resilient, diversified income streams.

Ongoing financial planning and adaptability are paramount to navigating economic changes.

Active Pursuit of Personal Aspirations:

Retirement becomes an opportunity for self-discovery and the pursuit of long-neglected passions.

A time to explore hobbies, travel, and engage in meaningful activities that contribute to a fulfilling life.

Entrepreneurial Ventures and Side Hustles:

The new retiree may embark on entrepreneurial ventures, leveraging skills and experiences for business opportunities. Side hustles and creative pursuits contribute not only to income but also to a sense of purpose and accomplishment.

Lifelong Learning and Skill Development:

Retirement is a phase of continual growth, with a focus on learning new skills and staying relevant in a rapidly changing world. Opportunities for education and personal development remain a central theme.

Technological Integration and Remote Work:

The utilization of technology allows retirees to stay connected, work remotely, and engage in global opportunities.

Virtual collaboration opens doors to new ways of contributing to industries or causes.

Health and Well-being as a Priority:

Retirement planning includes a holistic approach to health, wellness, and maintaining an active lifestyle.

Investments in physical and mental well-being are integral to enjoying the retirement years.

Social Impact and Community Involvement:

Retirees actively seek ways to make a positive impact on their communities and contribute to social causes.

Volunteering, mentorship, and philanthropy become integral components of retirement.

In this new paradigm, retirement is not an end but a beginning—a phase characterized by choice, purpose, and the ongoing pursuit of a meaningful and fulfilling life. It's about embracing
change, staying agile, and redefining what it means to live well beyond the traditional boundaries of retirement.

The role of passive income

Passive income is money that requires little effort to get. It includes revenue from rental properties, limited partnerships, and other initiatives in which you are not engaged in the ongoing generating of earnings. While these money-making projects may have needed your resources, time, or efforts at first, they usually pay off automatically and without you breaking a sweat.

The importance of passive income in the context of financial freedom and an ambitious retirement plan cannot be overstated. Passive income is a cornerstone, giving several advantages that contribute to a more secure and flexible financial future. Here are some essential characteristics of its role:

1. Financial Stability:

Passive income streams, such as dividends, rental income, or royalties, give a continuous supply of money, which contributes to financial stability.

2. Diversification:

Risk Reduction: Passive income diversifies your cash sources, minimizing your reliance on a single source of income. This diversity improves financial resilience during economic downturns.

3. Creating Wealth:

Asset Appreciation: Passive income often comprises assets, such as real estate or equities, which may grow over time, adding to total wealth creation.

4. Flexibility and Freedom:

Reduced Reliance on Employment: Relying entirely on active income from a job might restrict your financial freedom. Passive income allows you to pursue other possibilities, take pauses, or enter retirement on your own terms.

5. Aggressive Retirement Planning:

Passive income increases the building of retirement funds, allowing for a more proactive approach to accomplishing financial objectives.

6. Lifestyle Design:

Create Your Ideal Lifestyle: Passive income allows for a more purposeful planning of your post-retirement lifestyle. It allows you to maintain your preferred quality of life without being bound to a regular 9-to-5 employment.

7. Business Pursuits:

Facilitates Entrepreneurship: Passive income may be used to support entrepreneurial enterprises or creative pursuits, enabling retirees to explore business options without depending entirely on active income.

8. Time Freedom:

Time as a Valuable Asset: Passive income frees up time since it needs less day-to-day participation than active revenue sources. This time may be devoted to personal activities, hobbies, or meaningful time with loved ones.

9. Inflation Hedging:

Purchasing Power Preservation: Certain types of passive income, such as investments in assets that tend to grow with inflation, operate as a buffer against the eroding impacts of increasing prices.

10. Legacy Planning:

Generational Wealth: Passive income may help to create generational wealth, leaving a legacy for future generations. Passive income is more than simply an extra source of income; it is a strategic instrument that allows people to take control of their financial lives. Its importance goes beyond current financial requirements, and it is critical in developing a robust and proactive approach to retirement planning.

Embracing an aggressive mindset

Adopting an aggressive retirement attitude entails taking a proactive, smart, and empowered approach to molding your financial destiny. It entails deviating from traditional retirement standards and actively seeking a lifestyle that corresponds to your goals. Here's how to adopt an ambitious retirement mindset:

Redefining Retirement:

Beyond Conventional Thinking: Challenge typical retirement age expectations and embrace the concept that retirement is a stage of life marked by choice, purpose, and continuous progress.

Setting Bold Financial Goals:

Define clear and ambitious financial objectives for retirement. This might be specified savings goals, passive income milestones, or investment goals.

Aggressive Savings Techniques:

Contribution Maximization: Look for ways to increase your contributions to retirement accounts. Consider aggressive savings tactics to accelerate the development of your retirement nest fund.

Strategic Investment Decisions:

Balancing Risk and Reward: Take an educated and strategic approach to investing. Examine your risk tolerance, look at diverse portfolios, and examine assets that correspond with ambitious growth goals.

Continual Learning and Skill Development:

Lifelong Learning: Adopt a growth and development attitude. Keep up with industry developments, learn new skills, and be adaptive as economic environments change.

Entrepreneurial Spirit:

Taking Chances: Develop an entrepreneurial spirit via side hustles, business initiatives, or artistic projects. Utilize your abilities and expertise to investigate income-generating options.

Active Retirement Planning:

Regular Evaluations: Actively evaluate and reassess your retirement strategy. Make revisions depending on changing circumstances, objectives, and market conditions to ensure your approach stays aggressive and successful.

Prioritization of health and wellness:

Investing in Well-Being: Prioritize physical and mental health as vital components of an active retirement plan. A healthy lifestyle provides the energy and vigor required for an active post-retirement existence.

Work-Life Balance:

Developing Meaningful Routines: Consider a phased retirement strategy that balances work and leisure. Engage in activities that provide satisfaction while remaining linked to a professional or meaningful effort.

Networking and Collaboration:

Making Connections: Actively network and cooperate with others who have similar perspectives. Engaging with like-minded people may bring support, ideas, and possibilities for cooperation.

Adaptability to Change:

Navigating Transitions: Accept change as a constant and be adaptive to changing situations. An active retirement attitude entails negotiating adjustments with resilience and optimism.

In summary, a retirement adaptability attitude is about taking control of your financial future, setting lofty objectives, and actively constructing a retirement that is out of the norm.

It's a mentality that searches out possibilities, prioritizes continual progress, and puts you in control of your retirement experience.

SECTION II : UNDERSTANDING PASSIVE INCOME

Individuals seeking financial independence and a confident retirement plan must understand passive income. Once the initial setup is complete, passive income refers to revenues made with minimum effort or active engagement. Here are some crucial concepts to understand regarding passive income:

Passive Income Sources

Investment earnings include dividends from stocks, interest from bonds, and rental income from real estate.

Income from a firm in which you have little day-to-day engagement, usually obtained by employing management or automation.

Royalties: Fees paid for the use of intellectual property such as books, music, or patents.

Digital items: Revenue derived from the sale of digital items such as e-books, online courses, or software.

Inactive Participation:

Passive income requires initial work, time, or cash to generate the revenue stream. However, once established, the continuous commitment is modest.

Automation decreases the need for continual attention by using automation, technology, or managerial services.

Multiplication:

Diversifying passive income streams across many sources helps to decrease risk. The reliance on a single source is reduced, increasing financial resiliency.

Financial Stability:

Passive income often delivers a consistent and predictable financial flow. This consistency adds to financial security and may help with lifestyle choices.

Independence and adaptability:

Freedom: Passive income provides people with greater time flexibility, allowing them to pursue other activities, spend time with family, or even contemplate early retirement.

Assets for Construction:

Asset Appreciation: Certain passive income sources, such as real estate or equities, may grow over time, helping to enhance total wealth.

Tax Benefits:

Passive income may provide tax benefits, such as reduced tax rates on long-term capital gains or deductions for specific investments.

Active Management vs. Truly Passive Management:

Degree of Involvement: Some passive income sources may involve some administration or decision-making on occasion, but others are completely hands-off.

Strategic Planning :

Passive income options should be aligned with your financial objectives and risk tolerance. With careful preparation, you can guarantee that all of your revenue sources contribute to your overall financial well-being.

Constant monitoring and optimization:

Adaptability: Even though income streams are passive, they need frequent monitoring and modifications to adapt to changing market conditions, rules, or personal situations.

Understanding passive income is identifying its many sources, appreciating the initial work involved, and applying it strategically into your entire financial strategy. Passive income, whether generated via investments, company initiatives, or digital innovations, is essential for attaining financial independence and a confident retirement.

CHAPTER 1

THE ESSENCE OF PASSIVE INCOME

The core of passive income is the capacity to create revenues with little active participation, resulting in financial independence, flexibility, and a route to wealth building. The following are the key elements that determine the essence of passive income:

1. Less Active Participation

Freedom from the Time-for-Money Swap: Passive income frees people from the restrictions of exchanging time for money. Unlike active income, which requires constant work, passive income sources demand little to no continuing input.

2. Financial Independence:

Independence from Traditional Employment: Passive income helps people to reduce their dependence on traditional jobs. It allows you to pay your living costs, reach your financial objectives, and live a more independent lifestyle.

3. Risk Diversification and Mitigation:

Diverse Income Streams: Passive income supports diversification across several revenue streams. Diversification reduces risk and ensures that financial stability is not unduly reliant on a single source.

4. Wealth Creation:

Passive income often includes assets that might increase over time, adding to long-term wealth creation. Because of this, it is an essential instrument for achieving financial wealth.

5. Lifestyle Versatility:

Enabling Lifestyle Choices: Passive income allows you to make lifestyle decisions based on your own preferences rather than financial need. This might involve

retiring early, following one's hobbies, or traveling without the confines of a 9-to-5 work.

6. Predictability and stability:

Consistent Cash Flow: Many kinds of passive income provide consistent and predictable cash flow. This consistency improves financial security and gives peace of mind, particularly during times of economic uncertainty.

7. Time Independence:

More Time for Personal Pursuits: Passive income helps people to regain time for personal hobbies, family, and other activities. It allows for a more balanced and fulfilled existence.

8. Flexibility:

Potential for Growth: Passive income streams may be scalable, enabling people to diversify their sources of income and raise total revenue without raising work accordingly.

9. Tax Effectiveness:

Tax Benefits: Certain passive income sources may provide tax benefits, resulting in higher after-tax returns and overall financial efficiency.

10. Creating a Legacy:

Passive income has the potential to contribute to generational wealth, giving financial stability and possibilities for future generations.

The concept of passive income is founded in building a financial climate in which money works for you rather than against you. It's a way to reach financial objectives, enjoy lifestyle options, and eventually acquire a better feeling of financial independence and liberty

DEFINING PASSIVE INCOME

Earnings from activities or investments in which a person is not actively engaged on a daily basis are referred to as passive income. Passive income, as opposed to active income, which is obtained by direct involvement in job or company activities, needs less continuous effort after the initial setup or investment is in place. Passive income may come from a variety of sources, including:

Investments:

Dividend payments from stocks

Bond or savings account interest

Profits on the sale of appreciating assets

Property investment:

Rental revenue from real estate

Crowdfunding for real estate or investment partnerships

Ownership of a Business:

Earnings from firms in which the person has little engagement on a daily basis

Intellectual property royalties, such as those from books, music, or patents

Digital Goods:

Profits from the sale of digital items such as e-books, online courses, or software

Passive income is distinguished by the fact that, once created, it needs less direct time and effort to sustain than active revenue.

This allows people to be more flexible, pursue other hobbies, and even attain financial independence. It is crucial to remember, however, that attaining passive income often requires initial work, strategic planning, and, in some cases, financial commitment.

DIFFERENTIATING ACTIVE VS PASSIVE INCOME

The main difference between passive and active income is the amount of direct engagement or work necessary to obtain the money. Here's a summary of the significant distinctions:

Income from a Passive Source:

Limited Active Participation:

Once the initial setup or investment is in place, passive income may be made with little to no day-to-day engagement.

Continued Income Generation:

Even when the person is not actively working or managing the source, the revenue stream continues to produce money.

Passive Income Examples:

Dividend payments from stocks

Real estate rental revenue

Savings account or bond interest

Intellectual property royalties

Profits from automated or outsourced business initiatives

Freedom of Time:

Passive income allows for more flexibility and time freedom, enabling people to pursue other hobbies, travel, or engage in leisure activities.

Scalability:

Many passive income sources are scalable, enabling people to raise their profits without raising their direct work accordingly.

Active Earnings:

Direct Participation Is Required:

Active income is gained by participating directly in labor, employment, or company activities.

Without active work, income declines:

When a person is not actively working, active revenue ceases to flow. You do not get paid if you do not work.

Active Income Examples:

Wages or salary from employment

Earnings from actively operating a company

Fees for delivering services or consulting

Commissions on sales

Time-for-Money Exchange:

Active income often entails a time-for-money trade-off, with profits directly proportional to the amount of time and effort put in.

Freedom for a Limited Time:

Active income may give less flexibility since it involves continual engagement, making it more difficult to leave a job without losing money.

Once the initial job is completed, passive income demands less continuing effort, allowing for more autonomy and freedom. Active income, on the other hand, is gained directly via involvement in labor and ceases when the person ceases to work. Individuals often attempt to diversify their income

sources in order to build a balanced financial portfolio, and both types of income play various roles

IMPORTANCE IN RETIREMENT PLANNING

Passive income is essential in retirement planning for various reasons:

1. Financial Independence:

Passive income offers a consistent source of revenue, minimizing dependency on conventional wage income throughout retirement. This financial freedom enables retirees to keep their preferred lifestyle without being bound to a work.

2. Risk Management and Diversification:

Relying primarily on pensions or withdrawals from savings might be risky. Passive income diversified income sources, minimizing exposure to economic downturns or volatility in financial markets.

3. Stability and predictability:

Many passive income sources, such as dividends and rental income, provide a consistent and predictable cash flow. This steadiness adds to financial security, particularly in retirement, when a steady income is required.

4. Continued Growth and Wealth Preservation:

Passive income, which is often earned via investments, may help to ensure sustained asset development and preservation. This is critical for retirees who want their assets to survive their retirement years and maybe leave a legacy.

5. Flexibility and Lifestyle Design:

Passive income allows retirees to construct their own lifestyle. Passive income allows you to travel, pursue hobbies, or give back to the community without having to work.

6. Reduced Withdrawal Pressure:

Having consistent passive income sources decreases the need to make large withdrawals from retirement funds. This may assist to protect the life of investments and provide a more sustainable financial strategy.

7. Adapting to Changing Circumstances:

Passive income enables retirees to adjust to changing circumstances, such as unforeseen bills or economic adjustments. The resilience afforded by numerous revenue sources improves financial adaptation.

8. Inflation Protection:

Certain types of passive income, such as investments that outperform inflation, operate as a buffer against the eroding impacts of increasing prices. This helps to preserve buying power throughout retirement.

9. Legacy Planning:

Passive income may help to create generational wealth, enabling retirees to leave a financial legacy for their successors.

Embracing Early Retirement:

Passive income is often a critical component for people striving for early retirement. It allows for the payment of living costs without the requirement for regular employment, allowing for a more flexible and early retirement from the labor.

A solid retirement plan must include passive income. It provides financial security, flexibility, and the opportunity for continuous development, making it a crucial tool for retirees wishing to protect their financial future and have a meaningful post-career life.

CHAPTER 2

TYPES OF PASSIVE INCOME

Passive income may be created from a variety of sources, allowing people to diversify their cash streams. Here are some examples of frequent forms of passive income:

1. Income from Dividends:

Dividends from stocks are the source.

Mechanism: Earned by owning dividend-paying stocks, which provide a portion of the company's income.

2. Rental Earnings:

Real estate properties, such as residential or business rents, are the source.

Mechanism: Earned by renting out houses to renters.

3. Interest Earnings:

Interest on savings accounts, certificates of deposit (CDs), or bonds is a common source of income.

Interest is earned on money deposited or invested in interest-bearing securities.

4. Entrepreneurship:

Earnings from firms in which the person has little day-to-day engagement.

Mechanism: Owning stock in a firm, forming a partnership, or having a stake in its earnings.

5. Royalties:

Payments for the use of intellectual property, such as books, music, patents, or trademarks, as a source.

Mechanism: When others utilize or license the creator's intellectual property, the creator earns money.

6. Affiliate Marketing:

Earnings from affiliate programs that promote and sell goods or services.

Earn commissions on each sale or lead produced by affiliate marketing activities.

7. Peer-to-Peer Loans:

Interest made by lending money to people or small companies is the source.

Individuals serve as lenders and earn interest on loans made to others.

8. Digital Goods:

Earnings from digital items such as e-books, online courses, or software.

Customers buy or subscribe to digital items, which generates revenue.

9. Crowdfunding for Real Estate:

Returns on aggregated investments in real estate projects via crowdfunding platforms.

Mechanism: Funds are contributed by investors, and profits are dispersed depending on project success.

10. Stock Photography: Earnings from licensing photographs for use by others.

Photographers get royalties when their images are downloaded or bought.

11. Automated Business Opportunities:

Income made by firms that need little day-to-day engagement. Business procedures are automated or outsourced, necessitating less direct supervision.

12. E-commerce: Earnings from an online shop or dropshipping company.

Selling real or digital things over an e-commerce platform is the mechanism.

Diversifying passive income sources is a typical method for improving financial stability and resilience. Each sort of passive income has its own set of qualities, perks, and concerns, and people may combine them depending on their preferences, risk tolerance, and financial objectives.

Rental income and Real estate

Rental income is the money you make by renting out your home. It may be a terrific method to produce passive income, but before investing in real estate, you need to understand the dangers and advantages.

Real estate is land, as well as any buildings or other structures built on it. It may be residential, commercial, or industrial in nature. Real estate is a lucrative asset type that may offer income, appreciation, and tax advantages to investors.

Rental income and real estate are important Passive Wealth Guides.

Investing in real estate and collecting rental income is a tried-and-true method of accumulating passive wealth. This strategy provides a consistent cash flow, prospective appreciation, and the possibility of long-term financial stability. Here's a look at rental revenue and its relationship to real estate:

1. Making Rental Income:

The mechanism for generating rental revenue is to lease a property to tenants who pay monthly rent.

Consistent Cash Flow: This consistent stream of revenue gives financial stability by helping to fund mortgage payments, property upkeep, and profit.

2. Investing in Real Estate:

Real estate has the ability to increase in value over time, adding to total wealth creation.

Diversification: Investing in a variety of properties (residential and commercial) and locales may offer a well-diversified portfolio.

3. Property Types for Rental Income:

Single-family houses, apartments, or condos are examples of residential properties.

Commercial assets include office buildings, retail spaces, and industrial sites.

4. Important Success Factors:

Location: Buying in high-demand locations increases rental possibilities.

Market Analysis: It is critical to understand local real estate trends and demand dynamics.

Property management is important since it assures seamless operations, tenant satisfaction, and upkeep.

5. Leverage and financing:

Mortgage Financing: Many investors utilize mortgage financing to leverage their investment, enabling them to manage a greater asset with a lower initial outlay.

Risk Management: While leverage may boost profits, it also increases risk, particularly in a volatile market.

6. Tax Benefits:

Depreciation: Depreciation deductions may help real estate investors by lowering taxable income.

Tax-Free Cash Flow: Depending on the circumstances, investors may be able to enjoy tax-free cash flow via deductions and depreciation.

7. Problems and Solutions:

Vacancies: Vacancies may have an effect on cash flow; however, savvy marketing and tenant retention activities can reduce vacancies.

Maintenance Costs: Ongoing maintenance is critical, and planning for repairs helps to avoid unexpected costs.

Scaling and Portfolio Expansion:

Reinvestment: Reinvesting revenues in more properties allows for portfolio expansion.

Diversification: A well-diversified real estate portfolio reduces risk while increasing possible rewards.

9. Long-Term Wealth Development:

Wealth generation: Real estate, when combined with continuous rental income, may greatly

contribute to long-term wealth generation and financial independence.

Retirement Planning: Many investors consider real estate to be an important component of their retirement portfolio, since it provides steady income throughout their retirement years.

10. Community Benefit:

Community Development: Real estate investment may help to build a community by providing homes and assisting local companies.

Being a responsible landlord builds good connections with renters and increases property value.

The benefits of rental income

Passive income: Rental income may be a terrific source of passive income since you don't have to work for it after you've purchased the property and found renters.

Appreciation: Over time, real estate prices might rise, which means your home could be worth more than you paid for it.

Tax advantages: There are several tax advantages to owning rental property, including the opportunity to deduct depreciation and other costs.

The Risks of Rental Income

Vacancy: There is always the danger that your property may be unoccupied and you will be unable to collect rent.

upkeep: Owning rental property need constant upkeep and repairs.

Management: If you don't want to manage the property yourself, you'll have to employ a property manager, which will cut into your income.

Is rental income appropriate for you?

Rental income may be an excellent strategy to produce passive income and grow wealth over time. However, before investing In real estate, it is critical to do research and understand the hazards.

Here are some more things to think about:

- Your financial situation: Do you have the money to purchase a home and afford the upfront fees, such as closing costs and renovations?
- Your risk tolerance: Can you deal with the risk of vacancy, maintenance, and other issues?

- Your time commitment: How much time are you prepared to spend maintaining your property?

If you're thinking about investing in rental property, I suggest speaking with a financial adviser or a real estate agent for further information.

Rental income from real estate is an effective method for people seeking passive wealth creation. Successful real estate investment involves thorough study, strategic planning, and active management, but the benefits may go well beyond financial profits, impacting long-term financial stability and community growth.

Dividend Stocks and Investments

Dividend stocks are stock shares issued by corporations that distribute a part of their earnings to shareholders on a regular basis, generally quarterly or yearly. Dividends are a kind of distribution that may be a wonderful method to create income from your assets.

Investing in dividend stocks is a popular way to get passive income while also partaking in the stock market's growth potential. This strategy entails buying stock in firms that pay out a percentage of their income to shareholders as dividends. Here is an in-depth look of dividend stocks and their function in generating passive income:

1. Passive Income:

Mechanism: Dividend stocks pay regular dividends, usually quarterly, giving investors a consistent source of income.

Dividends are a percentage of a company's earnings that are delivered to shareholders as a reward for owning stock.

2. Dividend Stock Categories:

High Dividend Yield Stocks: These are companies that have a history of paying out higher-than-average dividends.

Dividend Growth Stocks: Corporations that boost their dividend payments on a steady basis throughout time.

Blue-Chip Dividend Stocks: Stocks in well-established, financially strong corporations that are recognized for paying out consistent dividends.

3. Investing Plan:

Long-Term Strategy: Dividend investing often corresponds to a long-term investment strategy, enabling investors to profit from compounding gains.

Reinvestment: Many investors opt to reinvest dividends in new shares, speeding the growth of their investment.

4. Dividend Investing Advantages:

Dividends offer a steady revenue source independent of market circumstances.

Dividend-paying companies have traditionally shown to be stable and resilient, even during market downturns.

5. Risk Factors:

Market Volatility: The value of dividend stocks might still fluctuate in the market.

Dividend reductions: During difficult economic times, corporations may decrease or remove dividends.

6. DRIPs (dividend reinvestment plans):

DRIPs enable investors to automatically reinvest dividends to buy more stock, compounding their holdings over time.

DRIPs often allow the purchase of fractional shares, which makes it simpler to reinvest dividends.

7. Variation:

Sector Diversification: To reduce risk, investors might diversify their dividend stock portfolio across many industries.

International Dividend firms: Diversifying your portfolio by investigating dividend-paying firms from other areas.

8. Tax Repercussions:

Tax Efficiency: Certain investors may benefit from reduced tax rates on qualified dividends.

Reinvesting dividends in retirement accounts may provide tax-deferred growth.

9. Research and Monitoring:

Company Health: Examine the financial health and performance of dividend-paying corporations on a regular basis.

Dividend History: A solid track record of stable or rising dividends is frequently a good sign.

Long-Term Wealth Development:

Compound growth occurs when dividend income and potential stock price increase combine to create long-term wealth.

Retirement Planning: Many investors include dividend stocks in their retirement portfolios since they provide recurring income throughout retirement.

Investing in dividend stocks may be a great approach for people seeking long-term wealth growth and passive income.

Investors must undertake rigorous research, diversify their portfolio, and evaluate their own financial objectives and risk tolerance, as with any investment.

Here are a few pointers to help you get started with dividend investing:

- Do your homework: Before investing in any stock, make sure you understand the company's operations, financials, and dividend history.
- Diversify your investment portfolio: Put your eggs in more than one basket. To

limit your risk, invest in a selection of dividend equities from diverse industries.

- Dividend reinvestment: If you don't need the income from your dividends, consider reinvesting them to acquire additional shares, which can compound your earnings over time.

Dividend investing may be an excellent strategy to produce income while also accumulating wealth over time. When it comes to investing, however, keep in mind that there are no guarantees. Before making any investment choices, always do research and thoroughly examine your financial objectives.

Business Ownership and Entrepreneurship

Entrepreneurship and company ownership are dynamic journeys that entail risks, creativity, and the opportunity for great rewards. Here's a thorough introduction to company ownership and entrepreneurship, whether you're establishing a tiny firm or growing an existing one:

1. Entrepreneurship Defined:

Entrepreneurship entails the development of new businesses, goods, or services, which is often accompanied by a willingness to take calculated risks.

2. Different Types of Business Ownership:

Sole Proprietorship: A single owner with complete control over all assets and liabilities.

Partnership: Shared ownership with others, with obligations and risks distributed.

Limited responsibility Company (LLC): A hybrid of a partnership and a corporation that provides limited responsibility and flexibility.

Corporation: A separate legal body with stockholders that provides limited responsibility but requires more sophisticated arrangements.

3. Establishing a Business:

Idea Generation: Determine a market need or opportunity and create a distinct value offer.

Market research involves assessing the target market, competition, and future demand for a product or service.

Create a complete business plan that includes objectives, strategies, financial predictions, and operational plans.

4. Entrepreneurial Characteristics:

Entrepreneurs have a clear picture of their objectives and are motivated by a desire to see their ideas realized.

Resilience: The capacity to overcome obstacles and disappointments is essential for business success.

Entrepreneurs must be adaptable to changing market circumstances, client preferences, and technical advances.

5. Economic Considerations:

Funding Options: Consider personal savings, loans, investors, crowdsourcing, or venture capital as funding options.

Budgeting: Create a realistic budget that takes into account initial expenditures, operations expenses, and anticipated cash flow issues.

6. Commercial Operations:

Legal Compliance: Ensure that all local rules, licenses, and permissions are followed.

Human Resources: Recruit and manage a talented staff while cultivating a happy and collaborative work environment.

Technology Integration: Use technology to improve operations, increase efficiency, and remain competitive.

7. Branding and marketing:

Create a powerful and unique brand identity that connects with your target audience. Develop efficient marketing tactics to promote goods or services and reach the target market.

8. Scaling and Expansion:

Strategic planning includes developing expansion plans, such as increasing product lines, entering new markets, or diversifying services.

Risk Management: Recognize and manage the risks connected with corporate expansion.

9. Adaptation and Innovation:

continual Improvement: To remain relevant in a volatile market, embrace a culture of innovation and continual improvement.

Customer input: Seek and use customer input actively to improve goods or services.

10. Legacy and Influence:

Consider long-term objectives, succession planning, and the possibility of making a lasting influence. - CSR (Corporate Social Responsibility): Use ethical corporate operations and donate to social or environmental causes.

11. Networking and Collaboration: Relationship Building: Develop strong networks with other entrepreneurs, mentors, and industry experts. - Opportunities for Collaboration: Collaborate with other firms or people to exploit complementary capabilities.

Entrepreneurship and business ownership need a mix of vision, perseverance, strategic planning, and flexibility. Successful entrepreneurs overcome obstacles, embrace innovation, and contribute to the business landscape's development and vitality.

SECTION III : ESTABLISHING A STABLE FINANCIAL FOUNDATION

Building a firm foundation is important in many facets of life, including relationships, personal growth, and business. Building a firm foundation is essential in all aspects of life, whether it is personal growth, relationships, or commercial ventures. Here's a detailed approach on laying a solid foundation:

In the sphere of personal growth:

Begin with a strong sense of purpose, identifying both short-term and long-term objectives, which will serve as a road map for your trip.

Define your beliefs and ideals, which will serve as the foundation for your choices and activities.

Adopt a continual learning mentality by remaining current on industry developments, broadening your skill set, and encouraging intellectual growth.

For long-term stability, ensure financial health via good budgeting, knowing income, spending, and savings.

Prioritize a healthy lifestyle that includes regular exercise, good eating, and mental-well-being activities.

In the context of interpersonal relationships:

To develop solid relationships, cultivate good communication skills that emphasize both attentive listening and clear expression.

Create a network of connections by interacting with others who have similar interests or ambitions and offering support and opportunity.

Develop emotional intelligence by understanding your emotions and building empathy in order to successfully negotiate interpersonal relationships.

In terms of time management:

To maximize productivity, develop excellent time management practices, prioritizing work based on significance and deadlines.

Encourage adaptation and resilience by seeing setbacks as chances for development and keeping open to change.

In terms of professional development:

Set strategic goals, dividing long-term objectives into attainable milestones, and rewarding accomplishments along the way.

Maintain honesty in all interactions, creating trust as a fundamental component of personal and professional relationships.

Keep up to date on technical breakthroughs in your sector, and embrace innovation as a contributor to long-term success.

Maintain legal and ethical standards in both personal and professional endeavors.

When it comes to self-care:

To avoid burnout, prioritize self-care while realizing the need of balancing work and personal life.

Consider the environmental effect of your activities and, when feasible, use sustainable approaches.

Solicit input from peers, mentors, or trustworthy advisers, and use constructive criticism to further your personal and professional development.

Building a strong foundation requires deliberate decisions, continual progress, and a dedication to concepts that connect with your beliefs. It creates the framework for a joyful and successful life journey in many areas.

CHAPTER 3

BUDGETING AND SAVING STRATEGIES

Budgeting and saving might be intimidating, but they're essential for gaining control of your plutocrat and reaching your fiscal objects. To get you started, consider the following strategies

1. Make a Budget Track Your profit and spending Begin by listing all of your yearly profit and spending. Charges should be classified into orders similar as casing, serviceability, food, transportation, and optional expenditures. Set attainable pretensions Set attainable budgeting pretensions that take into account both short-term and long- term fiscal bournes .

2. Emergency Reserve produces an Emergency Fund Set away a chance of your budget to set aside for unlooked-for costs or job loss. Three to six months' force For fiscal stability, end to accumulate three to six months' worth of living costs in your emergency fund.

3. Debt Administration Prioritize Paying Off High- Interest Debt If you have outstanding bills, pay off high- interest loans first to lower interest payments. Avalanche or Snowball Method Choose a debt vengeance option depending on your preferences and fiscal condition, similar to the debt snowball or debt avalanche fashion.

4. Savings robotization Set Up Automatic Transfers Set up periodic transfers to your savings or investment accounts to automate your savings. " Pay Yourself First" Savings should be seen as a non-negotiable cost, antedating optional spending.

5. Exclude gratuitous Charges Examine Yearly costs Review your budget on a regular basis to find and remove unwanted or optional costs. Bill Negotiation Work with service providers to get lower pricing on serviceability, insurance, and subscriptions.

6. Fiscal objects and Precedences Define fiscal pretensions Establish short- term and long- term fiscal objects, similar as copping a house, supporting council, or retiring comfortably.

Allocate plutocrat Direct your plutocrat toward particular objects, conforming your budget to your preferences.

7. Planning for the unborn Begin Early launch investing for the long term as soon as doable to take advantage of emulsion growth. Diversify Your Investments To successfully control threats, diversify your fiscal portfolio.

8. Insurance Protection Assess Insurance requirements Review your insurance content on a regular basis to corroborate if it's still applicable to your present situation. Probe Cost Savings to conceivably lower yearly payments, shop around for competitive insurance prices.

9. Examine and Acclimate Regularly Review Your Budget Review and amend your budget on a regular basis depending on changes in income, spending, or fiscal objects. Celebrate Financial accomplishments Commemorate fiscal accomplishments similar to debt prepayment or attaining a savings target.

10. Fiscal knowledge Prepare Yourself Continue to educate yourself on particular finance matters in order to make sound fiscal judgments. Seek

Professional Advice For acclimatized advice, consider speaking with a fiscal professional.

Putting these budgeting and saving ideas into action involves discipline, thickness, and a visionary station to fiscal operation. Reassessing your fiscal condition on a regular basis and modifying your strategy to changing circumstances will help to long- term fiscal stability and success.

Creating a Practical Budget

Creating a reasonable budget is a critical step toward financial stability and reaching your financial objectives. Here is a step-by-step method to creating a sensible and productive budget:

1. Determine Your Financial Situation:

revenue: Include all sources of revenue, such as wages, freelance employment, side hustles, and any other sort of money.

spending: Divide your spending into two categories: fixed (rent/mortgage, utilities) and variable (groceries, entertainment).

2. Monitor Your Spending:

Expense Tracking: Keep track of your expenditures for a month to see where your money is going. Use bank statements, receipts, or budgeting tools to get started.

3. Classify Your Expenses:

Identify recurrent fixed costs such as rent/mortgage, utilities, insurance, and loan payments.

List variable costs like groceries, eating out, entertainment, and discretionary spending.

4. Make Savings a Priority:

Emergency Fund: Set aside a percentage of your salary to create or replenish an emergency fund. This amount should be enough to cover three to six months of living expenditures.

Long-Term objectives: Prioritize saving for long-term objectives such as retirement, property ownership, or school financing.

5. Establish a Budget Framework:

Consider the 50/30/20 guideline, which recommends allocating 50% of your income to necessities, 30% to desires, and 20% to savings and debt reduction.

Budgeting using a zero starting point: Assign each dollar to a defined purpose to ensure that your revenue minus your costs equals zero.

6. Establish Reasonable Spending Limits:

Examine Your Habits: During the monitoring time, evaluate your spending patterns. Determine where you may save money without compromising needs.

Set Spending Boundaries: Based on your evaluation, set realistic spending limitations for each area.

7. Incorporate Debt Repayment:

List your debts: Include any outstanding obligations in your budget. Pay off high-interest debt first.

Avalanche or Snowball technique: Select a debt payback approach, such as the debt snowball or debt avalanche technique.

8. Make Use of a Budgeting Tool:

Budgeting programs: Budgeting programs such as Mint, YNAB (You Need a Budget), and others that automate monitoring and classifying costs should be considered.

Spreadsheets: For a more personalized approach, create a budget spreadsheet using programs like Excel or Google Sheets.

9. Examine and Adjust:

Review your budget on a regular basis to verify that it is in line with your financial objectives and lifestyle changes.

When faced with unexpected changes in income or spending, be flexible and adapt your budget as needed.

10. Maintain Discipline and Consistency:

Stick to the Plan: Consistently stick to your budget. Discipline is essential for budgeting success.

Commemorate Progress: To keep motivated, celebrate accomplishments such as completing savings goals or lowering debt.

11. Seek Professional Help:

Financial expert: If you need specialized counsel and direction, consider meeting with a financial expert.

Creating a workable budget involves dedication, frequent monitoring, and the ability to adjust as circumstances change. Customize your budget to reflect your financial objectives and goals, ensuring that it is a useful tool on your path to financial well-being.

Effective Saving Techniques

Adopting strategic tactics and building disciplined financial habits are required for effectively managing and expanding your savings. Here's a detailed tutorial to assist you through the process:

1. Define Your Short-Term and Long-Term Financial goals: Define your short-term and long-term financial goals, such as establishing an emergency fund, saving for a house, or preparing for retirement.

2. Create a Detailed Budget: Create a detailed budget that details your income, fixed spending, and variable expenses. This thorough analysis sheds light on spending habits.

3. Make Savings a Non-Negotiable Priority with "Pay Yourself First": Make saving a non-negotiable priority. Set up automatic

payments to a specified savings account as soon as you get your paycheck.

4. Establish a Sturdy Emergency Fund: Save three to six months' worth of living costs in a readily accessible account. This emergency fund acts as a vital safety net for unanticipated financial difficulties.

5. Examine and Reduce Unnecessary Expenses: Examine your spending patterns for unneeded or discretionary expenditures. Reduce non-essential purchases to make place for more savings.

6. Negotiate Bills and Expenses: Work with service providers to get cheaper prices on utilities, insurance, and subscriptions. Small savings on recurrent spending might add up to a lot over time.

7. Follow the 50/30/20 Rule: Set aside 50% of your income for necessities, 30% for desires, and 20% for savings and debt reduction. A systematic financial strategy is ensured by this balanced approach.

8. Use Windfalls Strategically: Instead of indulging in wasteful spending, use unexpected

windfalls such as tax returns or bonuses toward your savings objectives.

9. Monitor and analyze spending habits:

Use budgeting applications or tools to track your spending on a regular basis. Analyze expenditure habits to find places where changes might be made to save more money.

10. Exercise Restraint on Impulse Purchases: For large purchases, use a "sleep on it" strategy. Delaying impulsive purchases allows for more cautious examination of need.

11. Allocate a major amount of Salary Increases to Savings: When getting a salary raise, consider dedicating a major amount of the new money to savings rather than immediately boosting spending.

12. Take Advantage of Employer Benefits: Take advantage of employer-sponsored retirement plans, particularly if matching contributions are available. This is an efficient approach to save for the future.

13. Set Up Automatic Savings Transfers: Make saving easier by setting up automatic transfers to

your savings account. This regularity will help you stick to your financial objectives.

14. Establish different Savings Accounts: Create different savings accounts for specific purposes such as a vacation fund, a house down payment fund, or an education fund. This segregated strategy allows for targeted savings.

15. Review and adjust strategies on a regular basis:

Examine your budget and savings strategy on a regular basis. Make modifications depending on changes in income, spending, or changing financial goals.

By incorporating these tactics into your daily routine, you may increase your ability to save and strive toward a more secure and successful financial future. Successful savings management requires consistency, discipline, and a strategic focus on your objectives.

Emergency Fund Essentials

Building and maintaining an emergency fund is critical to your financial security. Here's a complete list of crucial factors to consider while building an emergency fund:

- To begin, realize the basic objective of an emergency fund: it acts as a financial safety net, providing protection against unexpected bills or income interruptions.
- Determine the amount of your emergency fund by saving three to six months' worth of living costs. This should include necessities like rent or mortgage, utilities, food, insurance, and any debt commitments.
- Keep your emergency money in a highly liquid and readily accessible account, such as a savings account, to ensure its accessibility. This ensures that finances are available when required.
- Create a separate savings account particularly for your emergency fund. This split helps to avoid unintentional expenditure and makes monitoring easier.
- Contribute to your emergency fund on a regular basis, even if the amounts are

little. Consistent donations over time will help to develop a strong fund.

- Set up periodic payments from your primary account to your emergency fund to automate your donations. This methodical technique provides consistent savings.

- Make contributions to your emergency fund a non-negotiable priority in your budget. Prior to tackling discretionary expenditure, set aside a percentage of your salary for savings.

- Review the amount of your emergency fund on a regular basis to reflect changes in living expenditures, income, or other financial conditions. Prepare to make necessary adjustments.

- Use your emergency fund only for true emergencies, such as medical bills, unexpected auto repairs, or temporary income loss.

- Select prudent and low-risk investments for your emergency fund. Safety and accessibility are more important than great profits.

- Develop financial discipline to reduce the need to use the emergency fund for non-emergencies. Use it only in cases when you really need financial support.
- Make it a goal to refill your emergency money as soon as possible after depleting it. This guarantees that it remains functional as a financial safety net.

Finally, improve your financial literacy so that you can make educated choices regarding your emergency fund and general financial well-being.

By including these factors into your financial planning, you can create a dependable emergency fund that will provide you peace of mind in the event of unforeseen financial crises.

SECTION IV : ROYALTY INCOME

Payments received by a person or corporation for the use of their intellectual property or assets are referred to as royalty revenue. This kind of revenue is often connected with creative works, innovations, or ownership of certain rights. Here are some important characteristics of royalty income:

1. Intellectual Property Types:

Copyrights: For the usage of copyrighted materials, such as books, music, movies, or software, royalties may be received.

Trademarks: Trademark owners may be entitled to royalties when others use their brand names or emblems.

Patents: Individuals or firms with patents may be paid royalties when others use, manufacture, or sell the patented innovation.

2. Royalty Income Source:

Royalties are often earned via licensing agreements, in which the owner allows others rights to use their intellectual property in return for money.

3. Original Works:

Books and Literature: Authors are paid royalties for each book sold.

Musicians get royalties from record sales, digital downloads, streaming, and public performances.

Movies and television programs: Actors, directors, and producers get paid royalties depending on contracts and agreements relating to the distribution and usage of films and television shows.

4. Inventions and Technology:

Developers of software get royalties from software sales or license agreements.

Inventions: Inventors may be paid royalties if their patented technology or goods are used.

5. Mineral and real estate rights:

Mineral Rights: Landowners may collect royalties if minerals or natural resources are extracted from their land.

Property owners may earn royalties by leasing their property for certain uses, such as telecommunications towers.

6. Franchise Commissions:

Franchisors get continuous royalty payments from franchisees in exchange for the right to operate under the established brand and business model.

7. Royalty Calculation:

Royalties are often computed as a proportion of the income earned by the use of intellectual property.

set Payments: Some contracts provide for set or minimum payments regardless of income earned.

8. Contractual Arrangements:

Terms and circumstances: Royalty agreements outline the terms and circumstances under which intellectual property may be utilized, as well as the length of the agreement and payment terms.

9. Additional Income:

Passive Revenue Stream: Royalty revenue is a kind of passive income since it does not need active participation in day-to-day activities to generate.

10. Tax Consequences:

Royalty Taxation: Royalty income is normally taxed, and tax rates vary depending on jurisdiction and the type of the revenue.

Individuals and corporations may earn a regular cash stream from royalties depending on the value of their intellectual property. For artists, innovators, and owners of valuable goods, it may be a significant source of revenue.

CHAPTER 4

INTRODUCING BOOKS AND EBOOKS

Exploring the Worlds of Books and Ebooks is a Journey for Everyone

Stepping into their universe is like opening a door to an infinite number of options. Whether you like the sharp turn of a page or the lit light of a screen, both provide an experience unlike any other. Let's have a look at what makes each one special:

Books:

- The tactile magic: There's nothing quite like holding a book in your hands. The weight, feel, and aroma of ink and paper all contribute to a sensory experience that computer forms just cannot mimic. Turning the pages is like beginning on a physical trip through the tale.

- Immersion reimagined: Books provide a deeper dive into storytelling. You become buried in the author's universe, uninterrupted by alerts or the allure of other tabs, allowing your imagination to paint the rich landscapes and infuse life into the characters.

Books are eternal treasures. They become treasures when passed down through generations, telling tales of the past and linking you to loved ones via shared memories.

The tactile connection: Studies have shown that reading actual books helps increase memory, attention, and understanding. The act of physically engaging with the text enhances the neuronal circuits involved in learning.

Key Points:

- Books come in a variety of genres, including fiction, nonfiction, mystery, romance, science fiction, history, and others.

Traditional books are tangible items, frequently composed of paper, having covers and pages that readers can turn.

Tactile Experience: Reading a physical book provides a tactile experience, engaging the senses via the feel of paper and the turning of pages.

Ebooks:

- Instant access to a world of stories: With a few clicks, you can carry a whole library in your pocket. Ebooks provide rapid access to millions of books, regardless of location or availability. No more trying to discover that precise title at the local bookshop!

- Convenience at your fingertips: Ebooks are very portable and lightweight. You can take your whole reading world with you, whether you're commuting, vacationing, or just relaxing on the sofa.

- Accessibility has been improved: Ebooks may be customized in terms of font size, color, and even text-to-speech, making them suitable for persons with visual impairments or reading issues.

- Many ebooks include interactive aspects such as notes, dictionary lookups, and even multimedia material, which enhances the reading experience in novel ways.

Finally, the decision between books and ebooks is a personal one. Consider your personal tastes, lifestyle, and reading habits. Perhaps you like the tactile experience of a physical book for deep dives into complicated storylines while embracing ebooks for on-the-go convenience and a fast dose of adventure.

Ebooks, or electronic books, are a digital progression of the classic book format. They are available on electronic devices such as e-readers, tablets, and smartphones. Ebooks are a simple and portable method to carry a large library, and they often include features such as changeable font size, search capabilities, and the option to highlight text.

Key Points:

- Ebooks are available in digital format, enabling consumers to read them on a variety of electronic devices.
- Portability: Ebooks allow users to carry a complete library in a single device, making them ideal for on-the-go reading.

Many ebooks have interactive elements such as hyperlinks, annotations, and search capabilities, which enhance the reading experience.

Common Ground:

Readers should consider the following:

- Personal Preference: Some readers like the tactile feel of owning a real book, while others value the convenience and conveniences given by ebooks.
- Ebooks enable rapid access to a wide library, but traditional books provide the pleasure of exploring via bookshops or libraries.

In conclusion, the introduction of books and ebooks emphasizes the many ways in which people may connect with literature. Readers may explore worlds, acquire information, and experience the thrill of storytelling in numerous media, whether they embrace the physical pages of a book or the digital convenience of an ebook.

- Whatever you choose, remember that both books and ebooks have the ability of taking you to other places, inspiring your imagination, and leaving you with tales that remain with you long after the final page is turned. So, choose a book or an ebook like the one in your hands and start reading!

The knowledge of online courses

Individualities looking to produce unrestricted income by participating with their experience, chops, and information have set up online courses to be a salutary resource. Here is a rundown of everything you should know about online courses in the environment of unresistant income:

1. The Rise of Online Education :The growth of online education platforms has changed the way individualities access literacy accouterments , making education more accessible to people each over the globe.

2. Implicit for Passive Income: Online courses give a unresistant profit since directors may make plutocrats from course deals without having to be laboriously involved in the course once it's established.

3. Platform Alternatives: individualities may produce and offer online courses via services similar as Udemy, Coursera, Teachable, and others.

4. Course Development Authors: produce course material by using their knowledge in a certain content area. Courses frequently contain videotape lectures, textual accouterments , quizzes, and interactive features. Structured Curriculum Courses are divided into modules or units to give a more structured literacy terrain.

5. Request Analysis: request exploration is frequently conducted by generators to discover demand for certain themes, assuring a potentially profitable followership.

6. Unresistant marketing: Once established, marketing operations similar as SEO optimization, social media creation, and chapter marketing might come dormant.

7. Scalability and robotization: Registration, material distribution, and pupil communication are all handled by robotization systems inside online course platforms. Scalability enables course inventors to reach a worldwide followership while reducing burden dramatically.

8. Content Diversification: Courses on subjects ranging from professional chops to particular growth may help generators gain unresistant plutocrats.

9. Monetization Strategies: One- time course purchases, subscription models, or a blend of the two may produce profit.

10. Interaction with Students: While creating the course requires some original work, nonstop involvement with scholars may be minimal, giving it a semi-passive profit source.

11. conservation and updates: Periodic updates may be needed to keep course material fresh, although these changes are constantly lower time- consuming than erecting a new course.

12. Learning Management Systems(LMS): Online course inventors may use Learning Management Systems to manage and deliver their courses more effectively.

13. Difficulties: contest As online courses come more popular, contests in certain areas may develop. Marketing In order to retain and retain scholars, strong marketing styles are needed.

By using knowledge and developing excellent educational material, online courses give a doable path for earning a sustainable income. Individuals may make sustainable profit aqueducts via online education platforms with strategic planning, smart marketing, and a fidelity to quality.

The Must know on Marketing and Launching
Marketing and releasing a product or service successfully requires a complete and planned strategy. Then is a comprehensive companion that covers all the bases Begin by doing expansive request exploration to more

understand your target followership, competition, and assiduity trends. Identify request gaps that your product or service can fill.

- Easily describe your Unique Selling Proposition(USP) to emphasize what distinguishes your service from the competition, stressing distinctive characteristics or advantages. Produce a thorough marketing plan that includes pretensions, target cult, channels, a budget, and a schedule.

- Consider both online and offline styles while developing a comprehensive strategy. produce a strong online presence by creating a professional website, social media platforms, and other digital channels. Use SEO to increase exposure and reach.

- As part of your content marketing plan, produce high- quality and useful material to gain trust and authority in your sector.

- Connect with your followership on social networking spots, post content, and produce a community around your business. conform your approach to the platforms that are most applicable to your target followership. probe influencer marketing by working with influencers in your assiduity or specialty to reach a larger followership and increase character.

- Produce and maintain a dispatch subscriber list for dispatch marketing, which will enable you to communicate with your followers directly, give updates, and promote special offers.

To enhance exposure and attract targeted callers, consider paid advertising juggernauts on platforms similar as Google Advertisements or Facebook Advertisements.

PASSIVE INCOME AVENUES

The appeal of unresistant income- making plutocrats while you sleep! There are innumerous paths to choose, each with its own set of pitfalls and prices. Let's look at some common choices Investing tips

- **Invest in stocks of enterprises** that pay out regular tips to insure a harmonious source of income. To limit threats, do thorough exploration and diversify your portfolio.
- **Own and rent out domestic or marketable parcels** to induce plutocrats from yearly rent payments. Significant original investment and continuing administration are needed.
- **REITs** Invest in a trust that owns and manages income- producing real estate, furnishing diversity and a reduced operation cargo than direct power. Fiscal instruments include Peer- to- peer lending
- **Earn income** by advancing plutocrats to people or companies using internet platforms. Threat evaluation and diversification are essential.
- **High- yield savings accounts** Invest your plutocrat in accounts that give lesser interest rates than regular savings accounts, giving a low- threat but limited- return choice.

- **Making content Blogging and monetization** Use a blog to make a followership and earn plutocrats via advertising, chapter marketing, or dealing your own goods or services. Harmonious trouble and followership participation are needed.

- **Ebooks and tone- publishing** produce and sell ebooks on internet commerce, entering royalties on each trade. To stand out in a congested request, marketing and branding are needed.

- **Indispensable strategies digital deals** Use internet requests to produce and sell online courses, templates, music, and other digital means. It takes time and trouble to manufacture high- quality particulars.

Consider investing in indispensable means similar to fine art, collectibles, or indeed granges, which may rise in value and give income via rents or deals. It requires specific moxie and involves a lesser threat. Flash back that there's no certain road to unresistant income.

Each choice involves disquisition, trouble, and careful assessment of your threat forbearance and fiscal objects. Diversifying your profit sources and carrying expert counsel as needed will help you succeed

Here are some other pointers to consider while deciding on a unresistant income sluice ;

- Determine your capacities and interests For long- term success, choose a choice that corresponds with your experience and interests.
- Determine your threat forbearance, Some druthers have bigger implicit prices but an advanced peril of loss.
- Before investing, determine your degree of comfort. Begin small and traditionally Do not dive headlong. Test several possibilities with bitsy deposits and gradually expand your unresistant income aqueducts.
- Seek professional advice For specialized suggestions and threat operation styles, consult fiscal counsels or specialists in certain diligence. Changing the stylish

source of income for you may be a fascinating quest. However, tolerance, and a different intelligence, If you approach it with knowledge

CHAPTER 5

RENTAL INCOME

It's a popular way to induce unresistant income, but it comes with its own set of enterprises, just like any other investment. Let's take a close look at the world of rental parcels.

Benefits Rent payments offer a harmonious source of income, maybe accelerating or indeed replacing your employment.

Property prices might grow over time, performing in possible financial earnings when you sell the property. Duty benefits Property possessors may abate mortgage interest, deprecation, and repairs from their levies. Affectation protection Rental income constantly rises in tandem with affectation, offering some protection against adding expenditures.

Challenges outspoken expenditures Purchasing a home requires a considerable original investment, which includes a down payment, ending charges, and indeed advancements. nonstop costs retaining a home entails nonstop costs similar as mortgage payments, property levies, insurance, keep, and repairs. Vacuities may have a big influence on your profit. operation liabilities

Managing a property on your own may be time-consuming, and hiring a property operation increases your costs.

Unanticipated circumstances similar as tenant damage, legal enterprises, or profitable downturns may have an impact on your profit and property value. Rental property types include

- Domestic settlements include single-family homes, apartments, condominiums, and townhomes. marketable property reimbursement includes office space, retail shops, storages, and artificial means.
- Holiday settlements are short- term settlements made available via companies similar as Airbnb or Vrbo.

Consider the following important factors:

Positions probe property valuations, rental rates, and vacancy rates in colorful points.

Property type: select a property that fits your budget, objects, and operation style. Webbing of tenants To reduce hazards, completely screen prospective renters. Repairs and keep Plan for regular conservation and be prepared for unanticipated repairs.

Legal and duty counter accusations Seek expert advice to comprehend applicable laws and regulations. Rental income may be an excellent strategy to produce wealth and earn an income, but it isn't without its difficulties. Careful study, medication, and fidelity are essential for success.

Basics of Real Estate Investing

Real estate investing entails the purchase, power, and operation of real estate for fiscal benefit. The following are the fundamentals of real estate investment

- Real estate investment types include Single- family houses,multi-family homes, and condos are exemplifications of domestic real estate. Office structures, retail spaces, and artificial spots are exemplifications of marketable real estate. Uninhabited property or parcels of land for unborn development.

- Investment ways Purchase homes for long- term appreciation and rental income. Fix and Flip Buying a property, redoing or enhancing it, and also vending it for a profit.

- Property Appraisal: It's critical to determine the worth of a property. Similar deals analysis, the profit fashion(for rental parcels), and the cost approach(relief cost) are all common methodologies.

- Flow of finances: A positive cash inflow is critical. In a perfect world, rental profit would surpass expenditures similar to mortgage payments, property operation freights, and conservation charges.

- Analysis of position and request: The value of a property is greatly affected by its position. Consider original trends, availability to installations, and general request circumstances. Due to industriousness and pitfalls Real estate investments are fraught with peril. Conduct complete due industriousness, including property examinations, title quests, and threat assessment.

- Property Administration: Effective property operation assures acceptable keep, tenant relations, and nonsupervisory compliance. Investors might resolve to manage their parcels themselves or employ professional property operation services.

- Counter accusations for Taxation: Real estate investments have duty consequences. It's critical to understand deductions, deprecation, and capital earnings levies in order to maximize gains. Appreciation Over time, parcels may grow in value, boosting their request worth. literal tendencies, profitable variables, and unborn development plans may all have an impact on appreciation.

- Exit ways: Have a distinct exit strategy depending on your investing objectives. Vending for fiscal earnings, keeping for continued rental income, or handing down to heirs at law are all options.
- Networking: Creating a network of real estate professionals, other investors, and assiduity experts offers significant perceptivity, possibilities, and backing.
- Considerations for the Law rebel with all original, state, and civil laws. Learn about zoning rules, tenant rights, and other legal issues that may affect your investment. Options for Backing research multitudinous fiscal choices, similar as typical mortgages, private lenders, and unconventional finance ways.
- Nonstop Education: Real estate requests change, and continuing education is essential. Keep up to date on request developments, funding openings, and assiduity stylish practices.

Real estate investing takes considerable study, strategic planning, and a long- term outlook.

Successful investors manage pitfalls, adapt to request changes, and continue to learn about the ever- changing real estate world.

Rental properties and Passive Income

Rental properties represent a prominent avenue for generating unresistant income, supplying investors with ongoing cash inflow while potentially profiting from property appreciation. Here is a disquisition of rental parcels and their part in unresistant income

1. Flow of Cash:

Rent payments from renters produce passive revenue for rental properties. When rental revenue surpasses operational expenditures such as mortgage payments, property management fees, upkeep, and taxes, the property has positive cash flow.

2. Appreciation Over Time:

Aside from immediate rental revenue, investors might benefit from the property's value increasing over time. Real estate markets can see expansion, which adds to the total worth of the property.

3. Property Administration:

While keeping a rental property involves work, many investors choose to outsource day-to-day obligations to professional property management services. This allows for a more hands-off attitude, which increases the cash stream.

4. Diversification:

Investing in rental properties provides a form of diversification within an investment portfolio. Real estate often behaves differently than other asset classes, contributing to risk mitigation.

5. Tax Advantages:

Rental property ownership offers various tax advantages, including deductions for mortgage interest, property taxes, operating expenses, and depreciation. These can positively impact overall financial returns.

6. Leverage:

Investors can use leverage by financing a significant portion of the property's purchase price through a mortgage. This magnifies potential returns while requiring a smaller upfront investment.

7. Passive Appreciation:

Property values can appreciate passively over time due to factors such as market demand, neighborhood development, or improvements to local infrastructure.

8. Tenant Stability:

Securing long-term, reliable tenants contributes to the stability of rental income. Investors can benefit from consistent monthly payments without the need for frequent turnover.

9. Real Estate Market Dynamics:

Understanding local real estate market dynamics is crucial. Factors like job growth, population trends, and economic stability can influence rental demand and property values.

10. Financing Strategies:

Investors may explore various financing strategies, including traditional mortgages, owner financing, or creative financing methods, to optimize returns and minimize upfront capital requirements.

11. Property Types:

Different property types offer various investment opportunities. Single-family homes, multi-family units, commercial spaces, or vacation rentals present unique considerations and potential returns.

12. Market Research:

Thorough market research helps investors identify areas with high rental demand, favorable economic conditions, and potential for property appreciation.

13. Risk Management:

Real estate, like any investment, involves risks. Investors should be aware of market fluctuations, potential vacancies, and unforeseen expenses, implementing risk management strategies.

14. Portfolio Building:

Acquiring multiple rental properties can contribute to building a diversified real estate portfolio, enhancing overall passive income potential.

Rental properties, when strategically chosen and effectively managed, offer a reliable source of passive income. Investors can benefit not only from regular cash flow but also from the long-term appreciation and tax advantages associated with real estate ownership. Careful planning, market analysis, and ongoing management are key components of a successful rental property investment strategy.

Managing a Real Estate Portfolio

Managing a real estate portfolio successfully requires a smart combination of financial acumen, organizational abilities, and a thorough awareness of the property market. Here is a thorough resource to help you prepare for the journey:

Portfolio Defined:

Property Type: Determine the emphasis of your portfolio: residential, commercial, a combination, or even specialist markets such as holiday rentals.

Risk Tolerance: Determine your degree of tolerance with probable variations in income and value. A well-diversified portfolio reduces risk.

Financial Objectives: Do you want a consistent income, long-term capital appreciation, or a mix of the two? Define your objectives to help guide your financial selections.

Key Duties:

Acquisition: Conduct research and select features that fit your plan. Analyze possible agreements by taking into account criteria such as location, condition, rental potential, and refurbishment requirements.

Financing: Obtain financing for your purchases via mortgages, loans, or other means. Examine interest rates, terms, and hidden costs.

Property Management: Determine if you want to manage your own properties or employ a professional. Think about your workload, time commitment, and expertise.

Tenant Management includes carefully screening possible renters, creating clear lease agreements, collecting rent, and dealing with maintenance concerns in a timely and professional manner.

Repairs and maintenance: Make a budget for regular maintenance and plan for unforeseen repairs. Negotiate with reliable contractors and prioritize required maintenance.

Maintain thorough records of your income, spending, capital upgrades, and loan payments. For complicated portfolios, use accounting software or employ a financial adviser.

Performance Monitoring: Analyze the performance of your portfolio on a regular basis. Maintain a record of vacancy rates, rental revenue, property valuations, and costs. Adjust your plan as appropriate in response to market developments and financial objectives.

Resources and tools:

Streamline operations, manage spending, and assess success using real estate investing software.

Data from market research: Keep up to date on real estate trends, rental prices, and local legislation.

Networks of professionals: Make contact with knowledgeable investors, property managers, and real estate brokers.

Legal and financial counsel: Seek professional assistance with complicated transactions, tax ramifications, and investment plans.

Problems and Solutions:

Vacancies: To reduce vacancy times, implement efficient marketing tactics, provide competitive rentals, and maintain high-quality buildings.

Tenant problems: Tenants should be adequately screened, clear communication routes should be established, and an eviction mechanism should be in place.

Unexpected maintenance expenditures: Set aside money for unanticipated maintenance costs and prioritize necessary repairs to prevent additional damage.

Market fluctuations: To reduce risk during economic downturns, diversify your portfolio across several locales and property kinds.

Remember that maintaining a real estate portfolio is a long-term commitment. For long-term success, be patient, keep educated, adjust to market changes, and always tweak your plan.

Important points

- Make contact with other real estate investors: Learning from their mistakes and sharing best practices may be quite beneficial.
- Keep current with legal and regulatory changes: Ensure that all applicable rules and regulations in your region are followed.
- Constantly educate yourself: To keep ahead of the curve, attend workshops, seminars, and study industry publications.

CHAPTER 6

STOCK MARKET INVESTMENTS

Investing in the stock market is acquiring shares or stocks in publicly traded corporations, which makes you a stakeholder and provides prospective rewards over time. Ownership kinds, investment methods, risk and return considerations, and order types are all important parts of stock market investing.

Stock exchanges, such as the New York Stock Exchange (NYSE) or the Nasdaq, allow investors to purchase and sell equities. The major forms are common and preferred stocks, with common stocks having voting rights.

Long-term investing, which focuses on a company's development and dividends, to short-term trading, which capitalizes on price swings, are examples of investment methods. Diversification, or spreading investments across many stocks and sectors, aids in risk management.

Fundamental analysis includes evaluating a company's financial health, profits, and management, while technical analysis identifies patterns using stock price charts. Some corporations pay dividends, which provide investors with a consistent source of income.

Limit orders are established at a certain price and executed when the stock reaches that price, while market orders are executed at the current market price. Initial Public Offerings (IPOs) are the first time a company's shares are made accessible to the public.

ETFs are investment vehicles that are traded on stock exchanges and own a diverse portfolio of equities. Setting stop-loss orders, for example, aids in the prevention of big losses.

Economic and market circumstances must be considered, as well as ongoing learning about market trends and global economic issues. Many successful investors advise for patience and the compounding impact of gains over time.

Investment in the stock market provides chances for capital gain, dividend income, and portfolio diversity. It does, however, include inherent dangers, so investors should perform rigorous research, remain educated, and match their investing plans with their financial objectives and risk tolerance.

Introduction to Stock Market Investing

Investing in the stock market is a dynamic and potentially profitable financial venture that entails purchasing and holding shares of publicly listed corporations. Individuals may participate in the ownership of firms via this kind of investment, possibly benefiting from capital appreciation, dividends, and general economic development. Here's an overview of the fundamentals of stock market investing:

Corporate Ownership:
You become a shareholder in a corporation when you invest in the stock market. Each share you possess indicates a piece of ownership, and you may have specific voting rights in the company's choices as a shareholder.

Investment Objectives:

Investors enter the stock market for a variety of reasons. These might include capital appreciation (the rise in the value of your assets over time), dividend income, and wealth accumulation for long-term financial goals.

Stock Categories:

Common stock gives you ownership and voting power in a firm. Preferred equities provide set dividends but do not often contain voting rights. Stocks may be chosen by investors depending on their financial objectives and risk tolerance.

Return and Risk:

The stock market has inherent dangers, but with more risk comes the possibility of greater gains. Investors achieve this equilibrium by diversifying their portfolios and investing in a variety of businesses and sectors.

Market Transactions:

Stock exchanges, such as the New York Stock Exchange (NYSE) or Nasdaq, are where stocks are purchased and traded. Companies list their stock on these exchanges in order to ease trading and give liquidity to investors.

Investment Techniques:

Long-term investing is keeping stocks for a lengthy period of time in order to profit from a company's development as well as broader market movements. Short-term trading focuses on profiting from price swings.

Technical and fundamental analysis:

A company's financial health, profitability, and total potential are all evaluated using fundamental analysis. To spot patterns and make investing choices, technical analysts examine stock price charts and trade volumes.

Dividends:

Some businesses pay out a part of their profits to shareholders in the form of dividends. Dividend stocks may offer investors with a consistent income source.

Risk Assessment and Mitigation:

It is critical to understand risks such as market volatility, economic downturns, and company-specific issues. Investors use risk-mitigation measures such as diversification and stop-loss orders.

Continuous Education:

It is critical for effective investment to be current on market trends, economic data, and worldwide happenings. Continuous learning assists investors in making educated choices in response to changing market circumstances.

Long-Term Prospects:

Many successful investors stress the necessity of having a long-term mindset. Holding assets patiently provides for the compounding impact of returns over time.

Individuals may contribute to the success of companies and the overall economy by investing in the stock market. While there are dangers involved, educated decision-making, strategic planning, and a dedication to continual learning may all contribute to a fulfilling investing experience.

Building a Diverse Portfolio

Diversification is the foundation of a successful fiscal portfolio. It's the practice of spreading your eggs in several

baskets to reduce trouble and increase your chances of long- term success.

Also it's a step- by- step system to creating a broad portfolio that meets your conditions
Understanding Diversity ; Do not put all your eggs in one handbasket!

- Spread your investments among asset types similar as equities, bonds, real estate, goods, and indeed unconventional means like art or cryptocurrencies.
- Diversify further within each asset type. Rather than leaning just on tech companies, consider investing in healthcare, consumer goods, financials, and other assiduity. Company Sizes and request
- Capitalizations Include a blend of large--cap, and small- cap enterprises. Each has a varied trouble- price profile, and diversification ensures you aren't excessively dependent on the success of any particular establishment. Investment Styles inquiry growth, value, tip, and income- acquainted investment strategies.
- This guarantees that your portfolio benefits from colorful request conditions

and meets your planned income or capital gain objects. Diversification ways Index finances and ETFs

- These passively managed finances follow broad request pointers, furnishing quick diversification at cheap cost. Ideal for beginners or those looking for low-conservation druthers, cooperative finances laboriously managed finances furnish professional selection of stocks or bonds within a specified theme or approach.

- Choose finances with diversified goods and a track record of success. Individual Stock Selection For educated investors who are comfortable with exploration and trouble, picking individual companies from colorful sectors and assiduity may further customize your portfolio.

- Consider the following trouble Forbearance assesses your degree of forbearance with request changes. Immature investors may generally tolerate further trouble in exchange for possible long- term gain, but those approaching withdrawal may prefer income and stability.

Investment objects ;

Are you looking for income, capital appreciation, or a combination?

- Align your asset allocation with your objects. Consider your investment period. Long- term objects allow for further trouble forbearance, whilst shorter time midairs may need a more conservative strategy. Flash reverse that diversification is a continual trouble.

- Review your portfolio on a regular basis and make changes as your objects, trouble forbearance, and request circumstances change.

- Other Suggestions Seek experts help Consult a fiscal counselor for technical suggestions based on your specific circumstances.
- Do not over- diversify. Too important diversity might weaken your results.

- Aim for a well- balanced portfolio with applicable diversity to control trouble while maximizing possible returns.
- Rebalance on a regular basis Reassess your asset allocation over time to guarantee it's harmonious with your objects and trouble forbearance. Your portfolio may be rebalanced by dealing outperforming means and copping underperforming bone

Creating a broad portfolio takes study, strategy, and constant variations. Still, the benefits of minimizing trouble and boosting long- term earnings make it a worthwhile investment. With this guidance and tools at your disposal, you can confidently navigate the investing terrain and produce a portfolio that works for you.

Long- term Investment Strategies
Long- term investing ways are your voguish abettors when it comes to accumulating plutocrat. They're concerned with long- term growth that can repel request oscillations and

lead to a stable fiscal future. Consider the following major strategies

1. Begin Beforehand Time is your most precious asset in long- term investment. The sooner you begin, the further time your investments have to compound, which means your earnings will expand vastly over time. Indeed, bitsy payments beforehand might add up to large quantities later on.

2. Invest on a regular basis. Don't stay for huge lump payments. Commit to regular investments, indeed if they're little aggregates each month. This instills discipline, smoothes out request swings, and precipitously increases your wealth.

3. Diversify Wisely It's critical to spread your eggs in several baskets. Do not doggy your expedients on a single establishment or asset type. Diversify your portfolio by investing in stocks, bonds, real estate, necessary means, and indeed different sectors within each class.

This reduces trouble and guarantees that your portfolio isn't susceptible to specific request downturns.

4. Marker Low- Cost Investments Reduce freights and expenditures that reduce your earnings. Passive indicator finances or ETFs are preferable to laboriously managed finances since they've lower costs and follow broad request pointers, assuring diversity.

5. Keep an eye on the long term. Do not be startled by request volatility. Short- term volatility is necessary, but long- term investment is concerned with the larger picture. Invest through ups and down and avoid the temptation to deal in fear.

6. Rebalance on a regular basis Your asset allocation will naturally alter over time as certain means outperform others. Rebalance your portfolio on a regular base to save your intended trouble- price profile and to assure that each asset class reflects your target proportion.

7. Set Up Automatic Deposits Set up automatic deposits into your investing accounts. This eliminates the incitement to predate payments and promotes stable growth over time.

8. Seek Professional Advice If you're dealing with a delicate problem or are unclear where to begin, hiring a fiscal counsel might be profitable. They may examine your unique conditions, trouble forbearance, and objects, and also make a customized investment strategy suited to your exact situation.

9. Educate Yourself In the world of investment, information is power. Keep up to speed with request trends, new investment opportunities, and lucrative improvements. To make knowledgeable choices, study fiscal news, attend forums, and partake in constant knowledge.

Long- term investment is a marathon, not a sprint, so be patient and disciplined. forbearance, discipline, and viscosity are demanded. Stick to your plan, avoid making emotional choices, and concentrate on the long- term end of establishing a stable fiscal future.

Following these tactics and customizing them to your own circumstances will help you achieve your long- term fiscal objectives.

CHAPTER 7

ENTREPRENEURSHIP AND BUSINESS VENTURES

Entrepreneurship and business initiatives are exciting and demanding fields loaded with opportunity. It is the place where ideas become physical realities, influencing economies and driving innovation. So, if you have an entrepreneurial spirit, let's dive into the fascinating world of establishing and creating your own firm!

Steps that every ambitious entrepreneur must take:

Finding an issue and a Solution: It all begins with a passion or an issue you feel has to be solved. Conduct extensive market research, identify your target customer, and guarantee your enterprise has a distinct value proposition.
Making a Business Plan: This roadmap details your company's objectives, strategy, target

market, marketing plans, financial estimates, and financing requirements. It's an essential document for obtaining investors and directing your expansion.

Selecting the Best Business Structure: Is your business a sole proprietorship, a partnership, a limited liability company (LLC), or a corporation? Each structure has legal and tax ramifications, so choose the one that best meets the objectives and goals of your enterprise.

Obtaining Funding: Explore several financing possibilities depending on your business's demands and stage of growth, such as bootstrapping, loans, angel investors, and venture capitalists. Remember that investors are looking for solid company strategies and committed entrepreneurs.

Putting Together a Competent Team: Surround yourself with competent people who compliment your abilities and share your vision. Delegate duties wisely and cultivate a collaborative atmosphere.

Marketing and branding: Develop a compelling brand narrative that speaks to your target audience. To reach out to prospective consumers, use digital marketing tools, social media platforms, and strategic alliances.

Adapting and Evolving: Be ready to change your plans as necessary. To overcome problems and capitalize on opportunities, listen to consumer input, be educated about industry trends, and embrace agility.

Building Resilience: Being an entrepreneur is a rollercoaster ride. To overcome barriers and accomplish your objectives, persevere through failures, learn from errors, and have a positive perspective.

Starting and Growing a Company: Starting and growing a company is a wonderful experience, but it also takes careful preparation, smart execution, and tenacity. Let's go over the important phases and factors for making your business dream a flourishing reality:

Laying the Groundwork:

- **Idea and Validation:** Identify an issue that needs to be solved and make sure your solution has a market. Conduct extensive market research, comprehend your target audience, and verify your proposal with surveys, interviews, and prototype testing.

- **Business Strategy:** Create a roadmap that details your objectives, strategy, target market, marketing plans, financial predictions, and financing requirements. This paper is critical for gaining investors and maintaining momentum.

- **Legal and financial framework:** Based on legal and tax concerns, choose the best company form (sole proprietorship, LLC, etc.). Set up your financial infrastructure (bank accounts, accounting system) and get the relevant licenses and permissions.

Getting Started and Reaching Customers:

- **Create a Minimum Viable Product (MVP):** Create a minimal version of your service to test with early users, collect feedback, and swiftly iterate.

- **Marketing and branding:** Create a powerful brand identity that is appealing to your target audience. To reach out to prospective consumers, use digital marketing platforms such as social media and content marketing.
- **Sales & Customer Acquisition:** Develop and implement successful sales tactics that are specific to your product or service. Concentrate on developing great client connections and offering exceptional customer service.

Scaling and expansion:

- **Analyze and Improve:** Monitor performance data on a regular basis, get consumer input, and modify your plans to improve your company model and promote growth.

Invest in your team and your infrastructure: Build a competent workforce with the skills and ability to handle operations and growth as your company expands. Invest in technology and infrastructure to help with growth and process simplification.

- **Options for Funding:** Investigate several financial possibilities (such as bootstrapping, loans, and venture capital) to support your expansion objectives. Secure the resources required to carry out your scaling plan.

Challenges & Adaptability:

- **Market volatility:** Be ready to adjust to shifting market circumstances and economic shocks.

In a competitive world, differentiate your product and remain ahead of the curve.

- **Funding and cash flow:** Manage your money wisely and create long-term income sources to support growth.

Remember:

- Passion and devotion are essential. Your journey will be fueled by your belief in your concept and resilience in the face of obstacles.
- Maintain your adaptability and flexibility. Prepare to adjust your plan as required in response to market input and learning.

- Create a solid network. Surround yourself with mentors, advisers, and other entrepreneurs who can provide advice and support.

Growing a company is a marathon, not a sprint. Accept constant learning, cherish minor victories, and endure in the face of adversity. You can convert your business ambition into a flourishing success story with a well-defined blueprint, smart execution, and a resilient attitude.

Passive Income from Entrepreneurial Ventures

The allure of passive income from business endeavors! It's the holy grail for many company owners, providing the flexibility and financial security to pursue other interests while your endeavors continue to create revenue. Let's look at some fascinating options for generating passive income via your business endeavors:

1. Creating Digital Products:

Ebooks and online courses: Create and sell ebooks, online courses, or video lessons in your field of expertise. This may be a one-time effort with continuing income creation. Software and applications: Create subscription-based software or mobile applications that give continuing value to consumers and generate recurring revenue.

Digital templates and printables: Create and sell downloadable templates, workbooks, or other digital goods related to your specialty.

2. Creating Content Audiences:

Blogging and affiliate marketing: Create a devoted blog readership and create revenue via advertising, affiliate marketing, or selling your own goods or services.

Create a YouTube channel with intriguing content to attract sponsorships, advertising money, or product placements.

Subscription-based newsletters or communities: Create unique information and insights for paying subscribers via dedicated newsletters or online communities.

3. Making Use of Existing Products and Services:

Subscription models: Provide subscription plans for continuing access to your goods or services, such as monthly memberships or recurrent consultation packages.

Automated services: Create automated solutions that provide value to customers without your direct participation, such as automated investing platforms or online scheduling applications.

If your company strategy is successful, try franchising it or licensing your brand and intellectual property to others.

4. Invest in Income-Generating Assets:

Real estate: Invest in rental properties that provide recurring rental revenue. However, this demands a considerable initial expenditure as well as continuing administration.

Peer-to-peer lending: Loan money to people or companies using internet platforms and earn interest on your investments.

Dividend-paying stocks: Invest in stocks of firms that pay monthly dividends, providing a passive income stream.

Remember:

- Passive income does not appear overnight. Building effective passive revenue streams takes upfront work, smart planning, and continual maintenance.

Not every firm is suitable for passive income.

- Analyze your unique venture and uncover areas that may be automated or scaled without sacrificing quality or service.
- Diversify your revenue sources. Don't depend exclusively on one passive income source. Spread your assets and income sources to reduce risk and maintain financial stability.

You may establish a more sustainable and gratifying company model by deliberately incorporating passive income methods into your current entrepreneurial operations.

Remember that study, preparation, and a combination of original thinking and savvy execution are essential for reaching your passive income objectives. If you have any specific queries or wish to learn more about certain passive income alternatives, please do not hesitate to ask. I'm here to assist you on your entrepreneurial path and transform your company dreams into reality!

Balancing Business Risks

Balancing company risks is a fine line that every entrepreneur must tread. It is about managing uncertainty and making smart choices to avoid possible pitfalls while capitalizing on chances for progress. Let's look at some crucial tactics for keeping your company on track:

Risk Identification, Analysis, and Prioritization:

Begin by outlining all possible hazards. Everything from financial limits and market volatility to operational obstacles and legal concerns is covered.

Examine each danger thoroughly. Assess the possibility of its occurrence and the possible financial and operational effect on your firm.

Risks should be prioritized depending on their severity and probability. Prioritize reducing the most significant hazards first, while taking into account the costs and resources required for each risk management plan.

Implement Risk Management Techniques:

Diversification means not putting all of your eggs in one basket. Diversify your product offerings, target markets, and income sources to disperse risk and prevent being too reliant on a single component.

Contingency Planning: Create contingency plans for various eventualities. Backup suppliers, alternate marketing outlets, and emergency finance reserves are all examples of this.

Strengthening Relationships: Develop good working connections with suppliers, partners, and customers. When confronted with adversity, these partnerships may provide support and aid.

Investing in Insurance: Consider different insurance choices, such as property insurance, liability insurance, or business interruption insurance, to reduce certain risks.

Accept Adaptability and Constant Improvement:

Keep track of your progress and adjust your strategy as appropriate. Because the business environment is continuously changing, be prepared to change your strategy in response to new knowledge and growing threats.

Encourage an open communication and risk-awareness culture inside your business.

Encourage workers to identify and disclose possible hazards, and build a collaborative atmosphere in which solutions may be produced together.

Educate yourself and your team on risk management best practices on a regular basis. Keep up to speed on developing trends, new risks, and risk-mitigation solutions.

Remember:

- Risk management is a constant effort. There will always be some element of uncertainty in business, therefore embrace the challenge and integrate strong risk management procedures into your company culture.
- Seek expert help when necessary. Don't be afraid to seek advice from experienced

entrepreneurs, financial consultants, or legal specialists on specialized risk management measures.

- Learn from your mistakes. Every obstacle is a chance to learn and improve. Analyze previous triumphs and failures to uncover trends and continually improve your risk management strategy.

By employing these tactics and establishing a proactive risk management attitude, you can confidently traverse the uncertainties of business and create a better, more robust future for your company.

CHAPTER 8

CREATING AND SELLING DIGITAL PRODUCTS

In recent years, the world of developing and selling digital items has flourished, providing an exciting channel for entrepreneurs and artists to reach a worldwide audience and create revenue. Here's a complete guide to navigating this dynamic area, whether you're a seasoned practitioner or just getting started:

Choosing a Niche and a Product Idea:
Choose a subject about which you are enthusiastic and have extensive expertise. This provides authenticity and helps you acquire a loyal following.

Market research entails analyzing current rivals and identifying market gaps or unmet demands. Concentrate on a certain niche and provide a distinct value proposition.

Product Ideation: Create a list of potential digital product forms that are relevant to your specialization and experience. Take a look at ebooks, online courses, video lessons, templates, printables, software, applications, and subscription-based models.

Creating and Developing Your Product:

Prioritize high-quality content that provides true value to your audience. If necessary, invest in expert editing, design, and production.

Consider the most user-friendly format for your material. For the best user experience, utilize engaging writing styles, clear video editing, or user-friendly software interfaces.

Platform Selection: Select the best platform for hosting and selling your goods. Online marketplaces such as Udemy, Skillshare, Etsy, and your own website with ecommerce features are popular possibilities.

Marketing and Product Launching:

Build anticipation via teasers, social media marketing, email lists, and early bird discounts prior to the launch.

Effective Promotion: To reach your target audience, use focused advertising, content marketing, influencer alliances, and SEO optimization.

Pricing Methodologies: Provide several price levels or subscription plans to accommodate a wide range of budgets and preferences. To spark curiosity, consider providing free samples or previews.

Developing a Customer Base and Maintaining Relationships:

Engaging material: Continue to generate quality material that compliments your product and promotes you as a specialized expert.

Community Building: Create engaging discussion forums, Q&A sessions, or online communities to engage and retain clients.

Outstanding Customer Service: To guarantee client happiness and excellent word-of-mouth, respond quickly to questions, give helpful assistance, and resolve any issues.

Additional Resources and Hints:

- Use online tools and resources: There are several tools available to assist with video editing, graphic design, email marketing, and analytics.

- Keep up with industry trends: To remain ahead of the curve, keep a watch on shifting formats, platform modifications, and marketing methods.

- Seek mentoring and assistance: Connect with other artists, participate in online forums, or speak with mentors to learn from their experiences and get helpful advice.

Remember that creating and marketing digital items involves commitment, effort, and ongoing education. You can develop a sustainable company and achieve success in this dynamic industry by concentrating on a value niche, creating high-quality content, and connecting with your audience.

Overview of Digital Products,

The digital world is bursting to the seams with opportunities, and digital goods are at the forefront of innovation and ease. Understanding what these goods are all about, whether you're a customer or an aspiring maker, will enable you to engage in this dynamic arena.

What exactly are digital products?

Consider items or services that you can access and utilize online, rather than in physical form. That is what digital things are all about! They offer a wide range of services, like as:

Ebooks, online courses, research papers, webinars, podcasts, music, and digital art are examples of information-based goods.

Productivity tools, gaming, instructional software, corporate applications, and mobile apps are examples of software and apps.

Templates, printables, icons, typefaces, stock photographs, and video effects are examples of digital assets.

Subscription-based services include streaming platforms, cloud storage, online fitness programs, and language learning.

Advantages of Digital Products:

Accessibility: Available 24 hours a day, seven days a week, with quick delivery and simple download.

Convenience: They may be used anywhere, at any time, and on a variety of devices.

Scalability: Creators may reach a larger audience without regard to geography.

Cost-effectiveness: Because of reduced manufacturing and delivery expenses, digital items are often less expensive than physical ones.

Flexibility: Creators may simply update and enhance their items without having to reproduce them physically.

Digital Product Difficulties:

Intangibility: Some customers struggle to understand the value of something they can't touch.

The internet market is huge, making it difficult to distinguish.

Copyright protection and illegal access are two issues concerning security and piracy.

Marketing and promotion: Effective digital marketing methods are required to reach the correct audience.

How to Participate in Digital Products:

As a consumer, you should explore the wide offers available on internet platforms, support producers you like, and make educated purchase selections.

As a Creator, you must first identify your specialization and skill, then create value digital goods, choose the appropriate platform, and apply successful marketing methods to reach your target audience.

Further Research:

- This is just a brief introduction to the intriguing world of digital goods. Remember that ongoing learning and exploration are essential for navigating this volatile terrain. You may learn more by:
- Exploring prominent platforms: Look into online markets such as Udemy, Skillshare, Etsy, or Gumroad.

- Following are some industry trends: Keep up with new formats, technology, and marketing best practices.
- Participating in the community: Join online forums, attend seminars, and learn from other artists' experiences.

Digital items have transformed our access to information, entertainment, and tools. You may become a wise consumer, a successful producer, or just an educated participant in this ever-changing ecosystem by knowing its essence, rewards, and problems.

online courses

Online courses have evolved into an effective instrument for learning and skill development, providing flexibility, accessibility, and a wide selection of topics to investigate. Whether you want to further your job, follow a personal interest, or just broaden your knowledge, there is an online course for you!

Advantages of Online Courses:

Convenience: Learn at your own speed and on your own time from any location with an internet connection.

Affordability: Often less expensive than conventional classroom settings, with a variety of pricing methods and scholarship options.

Explore a wide range of topics, from niche hobbies to professional development issues.

Quality: Take courses taught by world-renowned professionals and institutes.

Interactive Learning: Participate in forums, conversations, and joint projects with teachers and other students.

Popular Online Learning Platforms:

Udemy: Massive Open Online Courses (MOOCs) on a variety of subjects, ranging from beginner to expert.

Coursera: Provides professional development courses in collaboration with institutions and businesses.

Skillshare: Short, project-based seminars that are perfect for rapidly acquiring certain skills.

MOOCs and professional certificate programs from major colleges and institutes are available on edX.

Udacity: Offers Nanodegrees for job progression and focuses on tech-related skills.

Selecting the Best Online Course:

Determine your objectives: What do you hope to gain by attending a course?

Is it for personal curiosity, professional growth, or the learning of a certain skill?

Platforms for research and courses: Options should be compared depending on your requirements, price, and chosen learning style.

Examine course reviews, verify teacher qualifications, and preview course material.

Consider the following course format:

Look for courses with the appropriate depth, structure, and engagement (lectures, videos, quizzes, assignments, and so on).

Learn more about the instructor: Choose a course taught by a subject matter expert with a clear and engaging teaching style.

How to Get the Most Out of Your Online Course:

- Set realistic objectives and deadlines: To prevent falling behind, plan your study timetable and adhere to it.
- Take notes, participate in conversations, ask questions, and complete projects to help you remember what you've learned.
- Connect with other students: Join online groups and forums to network and discuss your experiences with other students.
- Seek assistance: If you need assistance comprehending the content, do not hesitate to contact the teachers or course support.

Remember that success in online learning involves commitment, self-discipline, and a proactive attitude. You may unleash the immense potential of online learning and accomplish your educational objectives by selecting the correct course, actively interacting with the content, and developing a support network.

Platforms for Selling

When it comes to selling online, there are several platforms to select from, each with its own set of advantages and disadvantages. The optimal platform for you will be determined by a number of variables, including:

What you're selling: Different platforms cater to various product kinds. Some focus on tangible commodities, while others concentrate on digital products or services.

- Your intended audience is: Where does your ideal consumer spend the most of their internet time? It is critical to choose a platform that is popular among your target population.
- Your financial situation: Some platforms charge monthly fees or a share of sales. Consider your budget and choose a platform that meets your budget.

- Your company's objectives: Do you want to make a fast sale, raise brand exposure, or establish a loyal consumer base? Different platforms cater to various corporate objectives.

Here's an overview of several major internet selling platforms:

For tangible goods:

Amazon is the world's biggest online marketplace, with a tremendous reach and built-in consumer base but higher costs and competition.

eBay: A well-known auction and fixed-price platform, perfect for one-of-a-kind or antique products, but with a lower average order value than Amazon.

Shopify: A popular e-commerce platform with configurable storefronts and good connectivity with other technologies, but a monthly membership charge is required.

Etsy: A growing marketplace for handcrafted and antique goods that attracts a niche client base interested in one-of-a-kind things but has limited reach for non-artisan products.

In the case of digital products:

Udemy: A renowned online course platform with a vast audience seeking professional growth and skill advancement.

Skillshare: Aimed for hobbyists and those eager to acquire new skills rapidly, Skillshare is ideal for shorter, project-based learning sessions.

Gumroad: A straightforward platform for selling ebooks, music, software, and other downloaded material, with cheap costs and direct consumer interactions.

Podia: A membership site and recurring income model that allows authors to form communities and deliver unique content.

In exchange for services:

Upwork: A freelancing marketplace that connects freelancers with customers for a variety of projects and continuous contracts, but with significant competition and a concentration on short-term engagements.

Fiverr: Provides small and fast jobs for reasonable pricing, making it ideal for novices or those with certain abilities, but it might result in poor project values.

LinkedIn is a professional networking website that includes job listings and the ability to interact with prospective clients.

Your personal website: Building your own website allows you total control over branding and user experience, but it takes more time and work to acquire customers.

Consider the following additional factors:

Payment processing: Make certain that the platform accepts safe payments and interacts with your chosen payment gateway.

Delivery and fulfillment: If you sell physical items, use a platform that provides efficient delivery alternatives for both you and your consumers.

Consider the platform's marketing capabilities and how you might reach your target audience inside that ecosystem.

Remember that there is no one-size-fits-all platform for internet retailing. Investigate your possibilities, take into account your individual requirements and objectives, and choose the platform that best matches your company.

Marketing Strategies for Digital Creators

The digital environment might be intimidating for artists, so don't worry! You may stand out from the crowd and attract your target audience with the correct marketing methods. Consider the following key strategies:

1. Understand Your Niche and Audience:

Define your market: Who are you making things for? What distinguishing feature do you provide? Concentrate on your area of expertise and appeal to a targeted audience.

Recognize your target audience: Investigate their demographics, hobbies, and internet activity. This allows you to adapt your content and marketing messages to them.

2. The King, Queen, and Everything in Between is Content:

Create high-quality material: Whether it's videos, podcasts, blog entries, or social media updates, concentrate on providing interesting, educational, and helpful information that your audience will like.

Maintain consistency: Regularly post fresh material to keep your audience interested and demonstrate your commitment to offering unique insights.

Experiment with several formats: Mix up your content genres to keep things interesting and to appeal to a wide range of tastes. Consider video clips, behind-the-scenes peeks, Q&A sessions, or collaborations.

3. Make Use of Social Media Power:

Select the appropriate platforms: Concentrate on social media platforms where your target audience spends the majority of their time. Instagram is great for pictures, Twitter is great for real-time updates, YouTube is great for long-form material, and so on.

Improve your profiles: To attract organic reach, write intriguing biographies, utilize high-quality pictures, and include relevant keywords.

Participate actively: Post on a regular basis, reply to comments and messages, join discussions, and arrange interactive sessions such as polls or live streaming.

4. Create a sense of community and collaboration:

Network, collaborate, and cross-promote your material with other producers in your field. This broadens your reach and introduces you to new audiences.

Engage with your audience: Create a community for your brand. Respond to comments, answer questions, organize online challenges, and foster a feeling of community.

Participate in relevant online communities: join forums, groups, and conversations in your specialty to share your knowledge and interact with prospective admirers.

5. Search Engine Optimization and Social Proof:

Optimize your content for search engines by including relevant keywords and meta descriptions.

Encourage testimonials and comments: Positive feedback and word-of-mouth referrals may go a long way. Encourage fans to offer comments and share their experiences.

Use social proof: To illustrate your reputation and competence, highlight accolades, media mentions, or partnerships with well-known businesses.

6. Examine and Adjust:

Keep track of your progress: Analytic tools may help you better analyze your audience engagement, reach, and content performance.

Adapt your strategy: Don't be hesitant to try new ideas and alter your plan depending on statistics and audience response.

Keep up to date: To remain ahead of the curve in the ever-changing digital scene, keep learning about new trends, technologies, and marketing methods.

It takes time and effort to establish a strong internet presence. Be enthusiastic about your material, be consistent, interact with your audience, and be patient. You can cultivate a devoted audience and establish yourself as a successful digital creative with the appropriate methods and devotion.

SECTION V : RETIREMENT PLANNING STRATEGIES

Retirement planning might be intimidating, but with the correct tactics, you can create a safe and satisfying future for yourself. Consider the following crucial points:

1. Begin Early: The sooner you begin, the longer your money has to grow via compound interest. Even little early donations may have a big influence in the long term.

2. Define Your Goals: What sort of retirement lifestyle do you want? Do you intend to travel, enjoy hobbies, or assist family members? Setting objectives helps you calculate how much money you need to save.

3. Evaluate Your Current Situation: Determine your current assets, income, and obligations. This offers you a clear picture of where you are starting from and how much money you need to save.

4. Investigate Savings Options: Take advantage of several retirement accounts with varying tax benefits and contribution limitations. Typical alternatives include:

Employer-sponsored plans: 401(k)s and 403(b)s allow for tax-deferred contributions and are often matched by the employer.

Individual Retirement Accounts (IRAs): Traditional IRAs provide tax breaks, but Roth IRAs allow you to withdraw eligible contributions tax-free in retirement.

HSAs: Make tax-deductible contributions for eligible medical costs and enjoy tax-free growth and withdrawals if utilized for healthcare in retirement.

5. Make Smart Investments: Divide your funds across asset types such as equities, bonds, and real estate to diversify your portfolio and limit risk. Consider age-based asset allocation, which involves modifying your risk profile as you near retirement.

6. Estimate Your Charges: Look into normal withdrawal costs and make adaptations depending on your asked life. Consider affectation as well as prospective healthcare expenditures.

7. Examine and Modify: Readdress your strategy on a regular basis, particularly after important life events. Acclimate your objects, benefactions, and investments when circumstances and request conditions change.

8. Seek Professional Advice: Seek customized advice on particular investing strategies and withdrawal planning tools from a fiscal counsel.

Fresh Suggestions Pay off your debts High-interest debt may have a major effect on your finances. Prioritize debt prepayment before or in addition to withdrawal payments.

Live within your means As your plutocrat grows, avoid life affectation. Increase your savings rate to meet your withdrawal objects sooner.

Benefits should be maximized Examine your employer's withdrawal gratuities, similar as health insurance or matched benefactions. Consider Social Security and any other prospective withdrawal income sources. Have fun on your trip. Do not let withdrawal planning overwhelm you.

Find styles to make saving and investing fun, learn new effects along the way, and plan for a safe and satisfying future. Retirement planning is an ever- changing process. You can take charge of your future and produce an affable and meaningful withdrawal experience by beginning beforehand, making realistic objects, and using available coffers.

CHAPTER 9

SETTING RETIREMENT PRETENSIONS

Setting specific and attainable withdrawal objects is critical for a happy and financially secure future. Then there are some ways to get you started

1. Establish Your Vision: Consider your dream withdrawal life Where would you want to live? What kinds of conditioning do you wish to engage in? This assists in determining your fiscal conditions and life objects. Consider your life stages: Will you emphasize trips beforehand, and also reduce and concentrate on healthcare later on? Organizing your withdrawal into stages clarifies your objects.

2. Determine Your requirements: Calculate your yearly living charges Acclimate your being spending for affectation and projected healthcare costs. Consider intended passages, pursuits, and life advancements.

Estimate your profit sources Include Social Security, anticipated pension payments, rental income, and any other prospective withdrawal cash sources

3. Determine the Gap: Abate your anticipated profit from your projected costs. This indicates the monthly fiscal gap that you must close via savings and investments.

4. Establishing SMART objects specifically easily describes your objectives: similar as" accumulate$ 1 million for a comfortable withdrawal by the age of 65." Measurable Use measurable measures to track your progress, similar to yearly savings rate or investment returns.

Attainable Establish attainable objectives grounded on your income, earning implicit, and threat forbearance. Make sure your objectives are applicable to your asked life and values.

Time- bound Set timelines for your objectives, similar as attaining$ 500,000 by the age of 55.

5.Produce a Savings Plan: Determine your savings tools Employer- patronized plans, IRAs, and other duty- advantaged choices should be considered. Select an investing strategy grounded on your threat forbearance and withdrawal schedule.

Divide your coffers across different means similar as stocks, bonds, and real estate. Plan automatic benefactions Set up automatic benefactions to your withdrawal accounts to help you save more constantly

6. Acclimatize and Cover Progress: Circumstances in life change, Review and modernize your objectives and savings strategy on a regular basis depending on income variations, professional advancements, or family changes. Keep an eye on your investments.

Cover your portfolio's performance and acclimate means on a regular basis to save your chosen threat profile. Mark important anniversaries To keep motivated and on track, award yourself for important accomplishments.

Setting withdrawal objects is a nonstop process. It's a nonstop process that requires inflexibility and rigidity. You may manage your fiscal path with confidence and construct a safe and satisfying withdrawal future by following these way and continually reviewing your progress.

Defining Retirement Goals

Defining your withdrawal objects entails further than simply statistics and fiscal targets. It's about going deeper and picturing the life you want outside of your working times. Then here are some questions to help you reflect and explain your factual solicitations

1. Time and Freedom Consider waking up hereafter with no work or duties.

- What would be your first step? This exposes your topmost bournes and interests, which may lead to trip plans, creative trials, or community participation.
- How important time do you wish to devote to recreation, pursuits, and particular development? Consider acquiring new chops, volunteering, or just engaging in rest conditioning free of job limitations.

2. Position and Way of Life

- Where do you see yourself settling down?
- Do you want to live in a busy megalopolis, a calm sand city, or an antique mountain retreat? Consider the ideal climate, availability of loved bones , and access to wildlife.
- What type of diurnal routine do you prefer?
- Yoga in the mornings, gardening in the afterlife, and artistic conditioning in the gloamings?

Define your perfect diurnal schedule and the conditioning that would make you happy.

3. Connections and connections

- Who do you want to spend further time with once you retire?

This might be family, musketeers, or recently established groups with common interests. The capability to plan conditioning and peregrination around these connections becomes a significant motivator.

- What do you wish to give back to your community?

Consider volunteering, mentoring, or launching programs that reflect your principles and interests. Making a difference may enhance your withdrawal experience.

4. Personal Development and Legacy:

- What bents or moxie would you want to gain in withdrawal? Learning a new language, taking art assignments, or sharing in tone- discovery forums may keep your mind active and help you achieve a continuance thing.
- What kind of heritage do you wish to leave?

This might be via family recollections, community sweats, or just living a life full of purpose and pleasure. Defining your heritage might help you make better opinions and stay motivated. Flash back that your withdrawal pretensions are special and one- of-a-kind. There are no right or wrong answers, and your vision may change over time.

Accept the process of reflection, write down your dreams, and use them to collude your path to a further meaningful future.

Assessing Financial Needs

Assessing your retirement financial requirements is a critical step in achieving a comfortable and rewarding future. Here's a detailed approach to determining your financial environment and the tools you require:

1. Calculate Your Monthly Living Expenses:

Current costs: Determine your typical monthly costs for accommodation, food, transportation, utilities, healthcare, and discretionary spending.

Adjustments for inflation: To anticipate your future spending, provide an approximate yearly inflation rate.

Adjustments to your retirement lifestyle: Think about desired changes in your lifestyle, such as travel, hobbies, or downsizing, and modify your costs appropriately.

2. Determine Your Potential Earning Sources:

Social Security: Based on your salary history and retirement age, calculate your estimated Social Security payouts.

Pensions: Include any planned pension income from your work or government schemes, if relevant.

Income from investments: Estimate the prospective returns from your current investment portfolio based on its previous performance and risk tolerance.

Rental revenue: If you own rental properties, consider the expected net rental income.

3. Bridging the Divide:

Subtract your anticipated revenue from your anticipated costs. This displays the yearly financial gap you'll need to close with more savings and investments.

4. Consider Healthcare Costs:

Health insurance prices: Determine the typical cost of health insurance premiums for your age and desired retirement coverage.

Out-of-pocket expenses: Include probable co-pays, deductibles, and uninsured pharmaceutical costs.

Long-term care: Think about the potential of requiring long-term care and look into the pricing in your region.

5. Evaluate Your Debt:

Make a list of your current debts and calculate your monthly payments. Debt with a high interest rate may have a major influence on your budget. Prioritize debt repayment before or in addition to retirement savings.

6. Think about your risk tolerance and time horizon:

Your risk appetite: Determine your degree of comfort with various investing alternatives and their volatility potential.

Time horizon: As you get closer to retirement, you may want to assume less risk with your assets.

Resources and tools:

Retirement calculators: There are several internet calculators that may assist you in estimating your demands and prospective income sources.

Consult a financial adviser for individualized advice on investing strategies and retirement planning.

Remember that determining your financial demands is a continuous process. Review your estimates on a regular basis and adapt your strategy when your circumstances or market conditions change. You may navigate your way to a safe and joyful retirement future with careful preparation and proactive modifications.

Long-term Vision and Planning

"Long-term vision and planning" is a strong word that holds so much promise! To properly go into this issue, I need some additional background from you.

Are you interested in personal long-term vision and planning, business-related objectives, or something else entirely?

Once I have a deeper idea of your focus, I may give specific assistance and tools to help you:

- **Craft a convincing vision:** What do you aim to accomplish in the long term? What influence do you wish to have? Define your personal or professional objectives with clarity and desire.
- **Develop a strategy plan:** Break down your vision into practical tasks and

milestones. Consider timeframes, resources, and probable difficulties.

- **Stay motivated and adaptable:** Long-term objectives demand persistent devotion. I may provide techniques to keep focused, measure progress, and alter your strategy as required.

Explore related resources: Depending on your requirements, I may give you books, articles, tools, or even link you with specialists that can further help your path.

Remember, long-term vision and planning is a constant process. The more you interact with it, the clearer your path will become.

CHAPTER 10

LIFESTYLE DESIGN IN RETIREMENT

Creating an affable and meaningful withdrawal life entails further than just fiscal security. It's about imagining and designing a way of life that feeds your interests, fires your purpose, and provides you pleasure every day. Then there are many pivotal points to consider

1. Identify Your" Why" What's authentically important to you? What values and pretensions do you wish to pursue in your life after work? Is it travel, particular development, family time, cultural trials, or making a difference in the world? Discovering your primary motivators can help you make design opinions.

2. Produce a Dream Chart Consider your perfect withdrawal day: Where have you gone? What exactly are you doing? What are you doing? This visualization exercise assists you in relating the exact conditioning, interests, and connections that offer you joy.

3. Consider the setting and position: Do you want to live in a lively megalopolis, a peaceful country, or close to family and musketeers? Define your ideal setting and look into possibilities that fit your life and budget.

4. Discovering New Interests and Conditioning: Retirement is an occasion to revitalize your life! Consider trying commodity new things, similar to learning a new language, learning a musical instrument, volunteering, or beginning a creative design. Accept curiosity and seek out new ways to express yourself.

5. Establish Meaningful connections: Retirement doesn't have to be lonesome. connections with family and musketeers should be prioritized. Consider joining clubs, levy associations, or online communities that partake in your interests.

Develop social connections that keep you interested and give you a feeling of belonging.

6.Encourage Personal Development: noway stop developing and learning! Take advantage of learning possibilities similar to online classes, forums , and trips. Engage in intellectual conditioning that will engage your mind and keep you feeling reenergized.

7. Keep your physical and internal health in check: Make healthy habits a precedent for a long and active life. Regular exercise, balanced food, and stress- operation strategies all help to ameliorate your general well- being. Engage in effects that you like, similar as tromping in nature, yoga, or spending time with loved bones

8. Be adaptable and flexible: Life takes unanticipated turns. Accept nebulosity and be ready to acclimate your plans when circumstances change. Keep an open mind to new options and let your withdrawal adventure unfold naturally. Flash back that Retirement Lifestyle Design is a trip, not a destination. Enjoy the process of discovery, accept experimenting, and, most importantly, concentrate on erecting a life that's uniquely yours.

Balancing Work and rest

For numerous of us, changing a balance between work and pleasure is a continual battle. Still, it's a worthwhile hunt since it leads to advanced productivity, lower stress, and a stronger feeling of general well- being. Then there are some essential tactics for achieving that fugitive balance

1. Establish Your Ideal Balance

- What does" balance" mean to you?
- Is there an equal quantum of time spent on work and rest?
- Having well- defined boundaries?
- Prioritizing colorful tasks at certain times of day?
- Define your ideal balance so you can strive toward it.

2. Establish Limits and Communicate

Make clear distinctions between work and particular time. Inform your associates and operation of your plans and stick to them. Learn to say no to further work when you are formerly overburdened.

Effectively communicate your limits. Make it clear to others that your time is precious and that you value your particular life. Open communication may help to avoid misconstructions and produce reasonable prospects.

3. Effective Time Management

Work duties should be prioritized. Prioritize the most essential jobs first, also delegate or remove the less important bones . To increase your productivity during work hours, use tools and practices similar to time blocking.

Make the utmost of your time-out. Plan and execute effects that you actually like. Avoid random social media surfing or spending your free time with errands. Concentrate on conditioning that will both rejuvenate and inspire you.

4. Engage in Mindfulness and Self- Care

Maintain alert over your energy situations throughout the day. Take pauses, go for a walk, or meditate when you are feeling exhausted. Prioritize your emotional and physical well-being by engaging in conditioning similar to exercise, good diet, and enough rest.

Disconnect from technology on a regular basis. Take digital detox breaks to reduce stress and concentrate on the then and now. Spend time in nature, interact with loved ones , and do effects that make you happy outside of work.

5. Be adaptable and adaptable

Life may be changeable, and your optimal balance may vary. Be flexible in your station to shifting circumstances and precedences. Accept that some weeks will be further work- ferocious than others. Do not be reluctant to seek backing.

Talk to a therapist, career counselor, or life trainer if you are having trouble changing balance. They can give you specific counsel and support as you manage this problem. carrying work- life balance is a process, not a destination. There will be days when you feel more drawn to one side than the other, and that is just OK.

The thing is to be deliberate with your time, prioritize your well- being, and acclimate your strategy as necessary. You may construct a life that feels satisfying both inside and outside of work by applying these tactics and getting attentive of your requirements.

Travel and Leisure Strategies

Words that conjure up thoughts of sun-kissed beaches, dynamic cities, and undiscovered experiences. However, arranging a fantastic vacation and actually enjoying leisure time may be daunting at times.

Worry not, daring soul, because I'm here to provide some travel and leisure methods that will help you maximize your enjoyment while minimizing your stress:

Planning a Trip:

Define your vacation objectives:

- Are you looking for leisure, cultural immersion, exhilarating activities, or a combination of all of the above?
- Knowing your "why" will direct your destination and experience choices.

Compare and contrast:

- Investigate travel blogs, guidebooks, and internet reviews to find hidden treasures, compare rates, and plan your schedule.

- Use tools like travel aggregators and booking sites to locate the greatest bargains.

Embrace adaptability:

- Allow for spontaneous discoveries and unexpected meetings.
- Allow yourself some free time to get lost in the present and don't overschedule yourself.

Pack smartly:

- Choose comfort and adaptability before trends.
- Choose breathable, mix-and-match gear that allows you to quickly shift between activities and climates.
- Don't forget the essentials: sunscreen, travel adapters, and a good book.

Embrace local experiences:

- Look beyond tourist traps for real interactions.
- Learn a few native languages, taste the local food, and make friends with the locals.

Strategies for Leisure:

Disconnect to reconnect:

- Turn off your phone, move away from the screen, and immerse yourself in the present moment.
- Listen to the sounds of nature, taste the local cuisine, and be totally present in your environment.

Mindfulness:

- Make time for reflection, whether via meditation, writing, or just observing your thoughts and emotions.
- Leisure time is a chance to reconnect with oneself and develop insight.

Try out new hobbies:

- Learn a new skill, attend a course, or engage in an activity you've always been interested in.
- Leisure time is a rich field for personal development and discovery.

Connect with loved ones:

- Share experiences with family and friends, play games, have important discussions, and make lasting memories.

- Leisure is about more than simply individual happiness; it's about sharing delight and strengthening friendships.
- Give back to the community by volunteering your time while traveling or participating in local activities. Contributing to something larger than yourself might give your free time more purpose and significance.

Remember, travel and leisure are about creating experiences that improve your life and spirit, not merely checking locations off a list. Be open to new possibilities, welcome the unexpected, and enjoy every moment.

Some pointers for delving further into leisure strategies

- Find wonderful vacation places depending on your interests and budget.
- Make your own itinerary filled with one-of-a-kind experiences and hidden treasures.
- Discover off-the-beaten-path activities and cultural insights.

- Recommend applications and resources to help you plan and schedule your next trip.
- Find enjoyable hobbies and activities to fill your free time.
- You may co-create a world full of adventure and fun!

Sustaining Financial Independence

That ideal situation in which money becomes a tool for enjoying life on your terms rather than a chain tying you to the job. there is one thing to get there, but keeping there demands clever methods and adaptation. Consider the following essential concepts:

1. Review and refine your plan on a regular basis:
Reexamine your original objectives and requirements. Have they evolved? Do you need to change your income or spending habits? Reassessing your circumstances on a regular basis ensures that your strategy stays in sync with your changing life.

Keep an eye on your investments and portfolio performance. Rebalance your investments as required to retain the risk profile you choose and to respond to market circumstances. Instead of letting your money wander, be proactive in controlling it.

2. Diversify Your Earnings:

Do not only depend on passive income. Investigate other revenue streams such as freelancing, consultancy, asset rental, or royalties from creative projects. Multiple sources of income create a safety net and reduce reliance on a single source.

Maintain an open mind to new prospects. The workplace is continuously changing. To keep ahead of the curve, be open to acquiring new skills, pursuing entrepreneurial projects, or adjusting your present revenue sources.

3. Make lifestyle flexibility a top priority: Be ready to change your living environment and costs. Downsizing, moving, or adopting a minimalist lifestyle may drastically lower your financial demands and increase the sustainability of your independence.

Accept alternative living situations. Consider house-sharing, co-living communities, or digital nomadism to reduce your living expenses and increase your freedom.

4. Keep a Healthy Emergency Fund:

Unexpected costs are unavoidable. Maintain an emergency reserve to meet unanticipated expenditures such as medical bills, home repairs, or lost income. Ideally, have 3-6 months' worth of living costs on hand.

Regularly review and alter the amount of your emergency fund. Your emergency fund requirements may alter as your income and spending change.

5. Keep Ahead of Inflation:

Invest in assets that have outperformed inflation in the past. Over time, real estate, dividend-paying equities, and certain commodities may help safeguard your buying power.

Negotiate for increased pay or income modifications. As inflation increases, lobby for changes to your revenue sources in order to retain financial stability.

6. Put an emphasis on continuous learning and growth:

Keep current with financial trends and possibilities. The financial world is continuously changing. To make educated judgments, invest in educational materials, attend seminars, and keep informed.

Learn new skills and adjust to shifting market demands. Upskilling and broadening your skill set may lead to new income prospects and improve your employability if you need to return to the conventional profession.

Remember that achieving and maintaining financial independence is a continuous process, not a one-time event. You can manage the economic ups and downs and keep your independence in the long run by embracing flexibility, adjusting to change, and actively managing your financial well-being.

Additional advice

- Diversifying your sources of income
- Taking charge of your money and portfolio

- Choosing the Appropriate Size of an Emergency Fund
- Changing your way of life to save money
- Keeping up with inflation

CHAPTER 11

TAX EFFICIENCY IN PASSIVE INCOME

That ideal script in which a plutocrat becomes a tool for enjoying life on your terms rather than a chain tying you to your employment. It's one thing to get there, but staying there requires cunning strategies and inflexibility. Consider the following crucial generalities

1. Review and modify your strategy on a frequent basis

Reevaluate your original points and requirements.

- Have they evolved?
- Do you need to modify your income or spending habits?
- Reassessing your circumstances on a frequent basis ensures that your plan remains in tune with your evolving life.

Keep an eye on your investments and portfolio performance. Rebalance your means as demanded to maintain the threat profile you've chosen and to acclimatize to request changes. rather than letting your plutocrat go down, take charge of it.

2. Diversify Your Earnings

Don't calculate only on unresistant income. Probe fresh income sources similar as freelancing, consulting, asset leasing, or royalties from creative trials. Multiple sources of income give a safety net and lessen dependence on a single source. Keep an open mind to new openings.

The plant is always evolving. To stay ahead of the competition, be open to learning new chops, developing entrepreneurial ideas, or altering your current income sources.

3. Make life inflexibility a primary priority

Prepare to modify your living situation and charges. Downsizing, downsizing, or espousing a minimalist life may significantly reduce your fiscal requirements while adding the continuity of your independence.

Accept indispensable living arrangements. Consider house- sharing,co-living communities, or digital vagabond to minimize your living expenditures and ameliorate your independence.

4. Maintaining a healthy emergency fund
Unanticipated charges are necessary. Maintain an emergency fund to cover unanticipated charges similar as medical bills, home repairs, or missed income.

immaculately, have 3- 6 months' worth of living charges on hand. Review and acclimate the size of your emergency fund on a regular basis. Your emergency fund requirements may change as your income and spending patterns change.

5. Keep Ahead of Affection
Invest in means that have outpaced affectation in history. Real estate, tip- paying stocks, and some goods may help to cover your purchasing power over time. Negotiate for advanced payment or income adaptations. As affectation rises, advocate for adaptations to your income sources in order to maintain fiscal stability.

6. Emphasize ongoing literacy and development
Keep up with fiscal trends and openings. The fiscal world is always evolving. To make

informed opinions, invest in educational coffers, attend forums , and stay informed. Learn new chops and acclimatize to changing request requirements.

7. Upskilling and adding your skill set may lead to new income openings and increase your employability if you need to return to your traditional job. Flash back that gaining and sustaining fiscal independence is an ongoing trouble, not a one- time circumstance.

You can ride profitable ups and campo and maintain your independence in the long term by embracing inflexibility, conforming to change, and laboriously managing your fiscal well-being. further guidance.

Diversifying your sources of income taking responsibility for your finances and portfolio Choosing the Applicable Size of an Emergency Fund Changing your way of life to save plutocrats. Keeping up with affectation

Understanding Tax Counter Accusations

Understanding duty consequences might feel like a maze, but do not worry! You can comfortably cut the world of levies and make educated judgments if you have a clear roadmap and some essential perceptivity. Then there are a many crucial particulars to consider

1. Understand Your duty Bracket This is the proportion of your income that you owe in levies. Understanding your duty type allows you to calculate your duty due and make sound fiscal choices.

2. Fete Deductions and Credits Deductions lower your taxable income, while credits reduce your duty bill incontinently. probe possible duty breaks and credits for costs similar as casing, education, healthcare, and charitable benefactions.

3. Select the Applicable Form Status Your duty type and possible deductions or credits are affected by your form status, similar as single, wedded form concertedly, or head of ménage. elect the status that maximizes your duty advantages.

4. Fete Different duty Forms W- 2s, 1040s, and 1099s are common documents that give income and expenditure information for duty purposes. Learn about these forms and how they contribute to your overall duty picture.

5. Suppose About Getting Professional Help A duty counselor may be essential in complicated duty circumstances or large fiscal gambles. They can help you in maximizing your return, minimizing scores, and navigating complex duty regulations. Fresh Information Government websites

The IRS website and the website of your state's duty agency both include duty attendants, forms, and calculators to help you in understanding your duties and calculating your prospective duty burden. Consider employing duty medication software to simplify and assure the correctness of your forms. Flash back that comprehending the duty consequences is a continual trouble. Keep up to date on new duty rules and developments, and examine your duty approach on a regular basis to acclimate to changing fiscal situations.

Seeking Professional Guidance

Seeking expert advice may be a prudent and useful move in many parts of life, including your financial future. Here are some crucial scenarios when expert advice may be very beneficial:

Financial Planning:
- Retirement planning: A financial adviser may assist you in navigating the intricacies of retirement planning, such as evaluating your income
- requirements, selecting investments, and optimizing your retirement benefits.
- Investment strategies: Depending on your risk tolerance and financial objectives, a professional may create a tailored investment portfolio that meets your requirements and helps you reach financial stability.
- Debt management: If you're drowning in debt, a financial counselor can help you devise a repayment strategy and build plans for future prudent borrowing.

Tax Planning:
- Reduce tax liability: Tax regulations may be complicated and ever-changing. A tax expert can assist you in identifying deductions and credits, optimizing your filing approach, and ensuring you pay the least amount of taxes feasible.
- Estate planning: Considering your legacy might be difficult. A lawyer who specializes in estate planning may assist you in drafting a will, establishing trusts, and minimizing estate taxes to ensure that your assets are transferred according to your intentions.

Business and Career:
- Launching a company: Navigating the laws and financial elements of launching a business may be difficult. A lawyer and accountant can advise you on the appropriate business structure, tax consequences, and financial planning to ensure your company's success.

- Career advancement: A career coach or business expert may assist you in identifying your skills and shortcomings, developing a career strategy, and negotiating for promotions or compensation increases.

Personal Well-Being:

- Mental health: If you're dealing with stress, anxiety, depression, or other mental health issues, a therapist or counselor may help.
- Relationship issues: A couples therapist or relationship counselor may help you improve communication, overcome disagreements, and deepen your relationships.

Finding the Right Professional:

- Investigate and compare qualifications: Look for individuals with expertise in your particular area of need, and double-check their credentials and certifications.
- Seek advice: Obtain references from friends, relatives, or coworkers who have

had excellent experiences with specialists in your area.

- Schedule consultations: Meet with multiple experts to pick someone you are comfortable with and whose approach matches your requirements and expectations.

Remember that getting expert advice is an investment in your future. The cost of services may seem costly at first, but the value and peace of mind they may bring can be significant in the long term.

SECTION VI : FUTURE TRENDS AND ADAPTATION

The personal financial and investing environment is ever-changing, impacted by rising trends and shifting global dynamics. Several significant developments are set to affect how people handle their money in the future, and adaptability to these changes is critical.

1. Technological Advances: The use of sophisticated technologies such as artificial intelligence (AI) and blockchain is likely to reshape the way financial services are provided. For example, robo-advisors use AI algorithms to deliver automated, low-cost investing advice. Adopting and adapting to these technologies is anticipated to improve efficiency and accessibility in financial planning.

2. Impact and Sustainable Investing: The emergence of environmental, social, and governance (ESG) factors is changing investment environments. Investors are increasingly looking for opportunities that correspond with their beliefs, with an emphasis on long-term and socially responsible investing. Adaptation entails adding ESG elements into investing strategies, reflecting a greater understanding of the social and environmental consequences of financial actions.

3. Decentralized Finance (DeFi): Blockchain technology enables decentralized finance, which threatens conventional financial middlemen. DeFi provides options that may expedite operations and minimize costs, ranging from peer-to-peer financing to decentralized exchanges. Adapting to this trend entails investigating these decentralized solutions while also comprehending and mitigating the hazards connected with them.

4. Tailored Financial Solutions: The age of one-size-fits-all financial advice is giving way to tailored financial solutions. Financial advisers may adapt recommendations based on individual preferences, objectives, and risk tolerances thanks to advanced data analytics and machine intelligence. Adapting to this trend entails accepting individualized financial planning solutions that adapt to each individual's unique demands.

5. The Gig Economy and Flexible Income Streams:

The emergence of the gig economy and flexible employment arrangements has an influence on how people earn and save money. Adaptation entails devising financial methods to handle irregular revenue streams, maximize tax efficiency in gig work, and assure long-term financial stability in a changing labor environment.

6. Central Banks and Digital Currencies Cryptocurrencies (CBDCs):

The investigation of digital currencies, particularly those backed by central banks, is gathering traction. Adapting to this trend entails remaining up to date on digital currency developments, comprehending their consequences for existing currencies and financial institutions, and assessing their position in diverse investment portfolios.

7. Financial Education and Literacy: As financial instruments and investment possibilities become more sophisticated, the need for financial education is growing. To respond to this tendency, cultivate a commitment to continued financial literacy, use educational tools, and seek expert counsel to make educated financial choices.

8. Aging Populations and Retirement preparation: As the world's population ages, retirement preparation takes center stage. Adapting to this trend entails rethinking retirement strategy, adopting novel retirement products, and dealing with the financial consequences of greater life expectancy.

9. Cybersecurity and Data Privacy: As financial services become more digital, the necessity of cybersecurity and data privacy grows. Adapting to this trend entails developing strong security measures, being watchful against cyber threats, and maintaining safe financial information management.

Adaptation becomes a cornerstone of financial success while navigating the future of personal finance. Individuals will be able to succeed in an ever-changing financial environment if they embrace technology breakthroughs, incorporate sustainable investment concepts, and remain tuned in to altering financial landscapes. Continuous learning, adaptability, and a proactive approach to financial planning will be critical to maintaining financial well-being in the face of these new trends.

CHAPTER 12

EVOLVING PASSIVE INCOME OPPORTUNITIES

The personal financial and investing environment is ever-changing, impacted by rising trends and shifting global dynamics. Several significant developments are set to affect how people handle their money in the future, and adaptability to these changes is critical.

1. Technological Advances: The use of sophisticated technologies such as artificial intelligence (AI) and blockchain is likely to reshape the way financial services are provided. For example, robo-advisors use AI algorithms to deliver automated, low-cost investing advice. Adopting and adapting to these technologies is anticipated to improve efficiency and accessibility in financial planning.

2. Impact and Sustainable Investing: The emergence of environmental, social, and governance (ESG) factors is changing investment environments. Investors are increasingly looking for opportunities that correspond with their beliefs, with an emphasis on long-term and socially responsible investing. Adaptation entails adding ESG elements into investing strategies, reflecting a greater understanding of the social and environmental consequences of financial actions.

3. Decentralized Finance (DeFi): Blockchain technology enables decentralized finance, which threatens conventional financial middlemen. DeFi provides options that may expedite operations and minimize costs, ranging from peer-to-peer financing to decentralized exchanges. Adapting to this trend entails investigating these decentralized solutions while also comprehending and mitigating the hazards connected with them.

4. Tailored Financial Solutions: The age of one-size-fits-all financial advice is giving way to tailored financial solutions. Financial advisers may adapt recommendations based on individual preferences, objectives, and risk tolerances thanks to advanced data analytics and machine intelligence. Adapting to this trend entails accepting individualized financial planning solutions that adapt to each individual's unique demands.

5. The Gig Economy and Flexible Income Streams: The emergence of the gig economy and flexible employment arrangements has an influence on how people earn and save money. Adaptation entails devising financial methods to handle irregular revenue streams, maximize tax efficiency in gig work, and assure long-term financial stability in a changing labor environment.

6. Central Banks and Digital Currencies Cryptocurrencies (CBDCs):
The investigation of digital currencies, particularly those backed by central banks, is gathering traction. Adapting to this trend entails remaining up to date on digital currency developments,
comprehending their consequences for existing currencies and financial institutions, and

assessing their position in diverse investment portfolios.

7. Financial Education and Literacy: As financial instruments and investment possibilities become more sophisticated, the need for financial education is growing. To respond to this tendency, cultivate a commitment to continued financial literacy, use educational tools, and seek expert counsel to make educated financial choices.

8. Aging Populations and Retirement preparation: As the world's population ages, retirement preparation takes center stage. Adapting to this trend entails rethinking retirement strategy, adopting novel retirement products, and dealing with the financial consequences of greater life expectancy.

9. Cybersecurity and Data Privacy: As financial services become more digital, the necessity of cybersecurity and data privacy grows. Adapting to this trend entails developing strong security measures, being watchful against cyber threats, and maintaining safe financial information management.

Adaptation becomes a cornerstone of financial success while navigating the future of personal finance. Individuals will be able to succeed in an ever-changing financial environment if they embrace technology breakthroughs, incorporate sustainable investment concepts, and remain tuned in to altering financial landscapes. Continuous learning, adaptability, and a proactive approach to financial planning will be critical to maintaining financial well-being in the face of these new trends.

Adapting to Economic Changes

The dynamic nature of the global frugality necessitates a visionary approach in conforming to changes. Individualities and businesses likewise must navigate profitable shifts to maintain fiscal stability and subsidize rising openings. Then there are crucial strategies for conforming to profitable changes

1. Diversified Income Aqueducts counting on a single source of income can leave individualities vulnerable to profitable oscillations. Diversifying income aqueducts through investments, side businesses, or freelance work provides stability and adaptability in changing profitable conditions.

2. Nonstop literacy and Skill Development The evolving job request demands ongoing skill development. Investing in education and acquiring new chops enhances rigidity, making individualities more precious means in the pool.

3. Emergency Fund Planning profitable misgivings punctuate the significance of having an emergency fund. A fiscal safety net provides a buffer during unanticipated events, similar to job loss or profitable downturns.

4. Flexible Budgeting Adaptable budgeting allows for adaptations in response to profitable changes. Prioritize essential charges, review optional spending, and identify areas where costs can be reduced during spare ages.

5. Entrepreneurial Mindset Cultivating an entrepreneurial mindset encourages individualities to identify openings amid profitable challenges. This may involve exploring tone- employment, starting a small business, or pursuing innovative gambles.

6. Networking and Relationship Building erecting a robust professional network enhances adaptability in the face of profitable changes. Networking provides access to new openings, assiduity perceptivity, and implicit collaborations that can cushion against profitable downturns.

7. Stay Informed About profitable Trends Keeping abreast of profitable pointers and trends allows individualities to anticipate changes and make informed opinions. Understanding request shifts and consumer geste enables visionary adaption.

8. Debt Management Prudent debt operation is pivotal during profitable misgivings. Minimize high- interest debt, explore debt connection options, and negotiate favorable terms where possible to palliate fiscal pressure.

9. Invest Strategically Strategic investing involves aligning investment portfolios with prevailing profitable conditions. Diversify investments, consider protective stocks, and acclimatize asset allocations grounded on profitable vaticinations.

10. Estimate Career Trajectory - Periodically assess career circles and be open to recalibrating professional pretensions. This may involve acquiring new chops, changing diligence, or exploring indispensable career paths grounded on request demands.

11. Influence Remote Work openings - The rise of remote work provides inflexibility and the capability to tap into global job requests. Embracing remote work openings can offer adaptability in the face of localized profitable challenges.

12. Social and Environmental Responsibility - Consider the social and environmental impact of fiscal opinions. Aligning with businesses and investments that prioritize sustainability can enhance long- term viability and adaptability.

13. Agile Business Strategies - Businesses should borrow nimble strategies that allow for rapid-fire adaption to profitable changes. This includes flexible business models, effective force chain operation, and a focus on client requirements.

14. Government Assistance and Programs - Stay informed about government backing programs during profitable downturns. These programs may give fiscal support, training openings, or impulses for businesses and individualities.

15. Cerebral Adaptability - Cultivating cerebral adaptability is pivotal. Developing a positive mindset, rehearsing rigidity, and seeking support during grueling times contribute to internal well- being, which is vital for navigating profitable changes. conforming to profitable changes requires a combination of fiscal prudence, strategic planning, and a flexible mindset. By staying informed, diversifying strategies, and embracing openings for growth, individualities and businesses can't only ride profitable shifts but also thrive in the midst of query.

Emerging Trends in Income Generation

The changing work and technology environment is giving birth to new and inventive methods for people to create revenue. Adopting these developing patterns might lead to new possibilities and reshape established views of work. Here are some major revenue generating trends:

1. Remote and Adaptable Work:

The trend to remote labor, aided by technology improvements, enables workers to contribute to businesses and projects from nearly any location. Platforms and solutions that enable remote collaboration are becoming an essential part of contemporary work.

2. Platforms for the Gig Economy:

Platforms for the gig economy are expanding, creating possibilities for freelancers and independent contractors. Individuals may use these platforms for flexible and on-demand labor ranging from ride-sharing and food delivery to freelance writing and graphic design.

3. E-commerce and online marketplaces:

Individuals may monetise their talents, goods, and services due to the simplicity of putting up online storefronts and marketplaces. E-commerce platforms provide innovators, craftspeople, and entrepreneurs with a direct path to a worldwide audience.

4. Subscription-Based Business Models:

Subscription-based revenue models are becoming more popular in a variety of sectors. Subscriptions for content, software, and services offer artists and companies with a regular income stream.

5. Collaborative Economy and Service Sharing:

The collaborative economy, characterized by the sharing of resources and services, has created new employment prospects. Individuals may contribute to a more sustainable and cost-effective way of life by renting out assets, providing services, or participating in collaborative consumption models.

6. Content Monetization and Influencer Marketing:

Brand partnerships, sponsorships, and content monetization are all ways for social media influencers to monetize their online presence. Platforms include services like ad revenue, fan subscriptions, and virtual gifts, which generate cash for content providers.

7. Virtual Events and Experiential Learning:

Individuals may now monetise their skills, abilities, or unique products via online platforms, thanks to the emergence of virtual events and experiences. Virtual training, consultancies, and entertainment events have all emerged as potential revenue streams.

8. Micro-Entrepreneurship Based on Skill:

Micro-entrepreneurship platforms focused on specialized talents are growing. Individuals may create revenue streams based on their knowledge by offering specialized services or selling digital items.

9. NFTs and digital products:

The selling of digital items, such as NFTs (Non-Fungible Tokens), is gaining popularity. Tokenization of work by artists, musicians, and producers provides unique ownership and financial potential via digital assets.

10. Services for Health and Wellness: Individuals with knowledge in exercise, nutrition, mental health, and holistic well-being may now earn a living because of the increased demand for health and wellness services. A burgeoning market is served by online coaching, courses, and specialized services.

11. Opportunities in Cryptocurrency and Blockchain:

The advent of cryptocurrencies and blockchain technology has enabled new revenue streams, such as bitcoin mining, staking, and involvement in decentralized finance (DeFi) systems. Through digital assets, these routes give alternate sources of revenue.

12. Green and Sustainable Income Opportunities:

The emphasis on sustainability has created revenue possibilities in green and eco-friendly businesses. Sustainable agriculture, eco-tourism, and environmentally aware goods help to generate money while also having a beneficial influence on the environment.

13. Augmented Reality (AR) and Virtual Reality (VR) Services:

Emerging technologies like AR and VR provide potential for people to earn money by providing specialized services such as virtual tours, immersive experiences, or instructional material in these creative media.

14. Education in Personal Finance and Investing:

Individuals with knowledge in personal finance and investing education will have more options as interest in these areas grows. Offering online classes, consulting services, or authoring financial literacy material has become a profitable business.

15. Consulting in Artificial Intelligence (AI) and Automation:

Individuals with experience in AI and automation might give consultancy services as these technologies become more widely used. Income is generated by assisting companies with

AI integration or by providing AI-based solutions.

Accepting these new trends requires a proactive attitude to learning, adapting, and exploiting technology. Individuals who investigate these alternatives have the potential to diversify their revenue sources, undertake passion projects, and manage the changing environment of employment and income creation.

Lifelong Learning for Continued Success

The pursuit of knowledge throughout one's life has become a cornerstone of long-term success in the fast changing terrain of the twenty-first century. Lifelong learning not only promotes personal development but also prepares people to manage changing industries, technology, and social dynamics. The following are major components of how lifelong learning leads to long-term success:

1. Technological Change Adaptation:

Lifelong learning is vital for keeping up with technology advances. Acquiring new digital skills and understanding emerging technology allows people to adapt to changes in the workplace and stay competitive.

2. Resilience and Flexibility in the Workplace:
Continuous learning fosters professional resilience by improving the capacity to pivot and adapt to shifting work markets. It provides prospects for job changes, promotions, and greater employability in a variety of sectors.

3. Problem-Solving and Innovation Skills:
Lifelong learners cultivate an innovative and critical thinking approach. Continuous exposure to fresh ideas and viewpoints sharpens problem-solving abilities while also encouraging creativity and flexibility in many parts of life.

4. Increased Networking Possibilities:
Engaging in continual learning allows you to connect with like-minded people, experts, and mentors. Networking within learning communities may result in beneficial collaborations, partnerships, and a larger professional network.

5. Improving Emotional Intelligence:

Lifelong learning includes not just technical skills but also interpersonal and emotional intelligence. Understanding human behavior, communication, and emotional dynamics aids in successful leadership and relationship development.

6. Higher Job Satisfaction:

Knowledge pursuit that is connected with personal interests fosters a feeling of satisfaction. As they match their employment with their interests, lifelong learners

frequently experience higher work satisfaction, leading to a more meaningful professional path.

7. Adaptability in a Changing Environment:

In a world of perpetual change, the capacity to learn and unlearn becomes critical. Lifelong learners demonstrate agility by swiftly adjusting to new knowledge, technology, and industry trends, guaranteeing their relevance in their chosen industries.

8. Defending Against Obsolescence:

Certain talents become outdated as industries progress. By proactively obtaining new skills that fit with changing work market needs, lifelong learning protects against professional obsolescence.

9. Lifelong Personal Development:

Lifelong learning extends beyond professional development to include personal development. Individuals who invest in their own well-being, emotional resilience, and interpersonal skills tend to enjoy more balanced and meaningful lives.

10. Enhanced Cultural Competence: Cultural competency is improved by learning about other cultures, views, and global challenges. This is crucial in today's linked world, since it promotes improved communication and cooperation in both personal and professional settings.

11. Adapting to Economic Changes: Economic landscapes may shift quickly. By obtaining the skills required for developing sectors, entrepreneurship, or other revenue sources, lifelong learners are better prepared to respond to economic developments.

12. Improved Problem-Solving Skills: Experimenting with different professions and disciplines broadens one's problem-solving ability. Lifelong learners may address issues with creativity and resourcefulness by drawing on a varied variety of information.

13. Developing a Growth Mindset:

A growth mindset—and mentality that views setbacks as chances for progress rather than insurmountable obstacles—is linked with lifelong learning. This mentality promotes persistence, resilience, and an optimistic perspective.

14. Creating a Learning Culture:

Lifelong learners often contribute to the development of a culture of continuous learning within their communities or organizations. They motivate others to take a similar approach by demonstrating the necessity of continual education.

15. Personal Empowerment:

Lifelong learning allows people to take control of their personal and professional lives. It fosters a feeling of agency, motivating people to actively influence their lives and follow their dreams.

To summarize, lifelong learning is more than just a professional requirement; it is a comprehensive approach to personal and intellectual development that creates the groundwork for long-term success in a continuously changing environment. Embracing a mentality of curiosity, flexibility, and a dedication to learning is critical to navigating the intricacies of the contemporary day and attaining long-term success.

CONCLUSION

Let us embrace the power of financial independence and the boundless possibilities that passive income may uncover as we complete the chapters of "Get Started: Passive Income, Retirement Adaptability," written by the perceptive James D. Lynn. Remember that the path to an ambitious retirement begins with a single step toward wise financial decisions.

It's more than simply a book; it's your road map to a more resilient future. The pages are loaded with tactics, advice, and a roadmap for an extraordinary retirement. The call to action is now loud and clear: seize these ideas, apply them to your life, and go on a path in which your money works for you.

Your bold retirement awaits. Allow your legacy to serve as the basis for the retirement you deserve tomorrow. Begin today, and let the next chapter of your financial success be inspired by James D. Lynn's inspirational words.

Begin now. Your retirement is deserving of nothing less than the best.

Dear Sir/Madam,

Remember that "Get Started: Passive Income, Retirement Adaptability" by James D. Lynn is more than simply a book; it's a road map to reshaping your financial destiny. It's now time to put your ideas into action.

1. Consider Your Financial Objectives:
Take time to consider your financial goals. What does your dream retirement look like? Clarify your objectives to provide a clear path for your financial journey.

2. Put one strategy into action today:
The book is jam-packed with tactics. Don't be intimidated; start small. Choose one method that speaks to you and put it into action right now. Small steps may lead to big improvements.

3. Participate in Continuous Learning:
A major topic is lifelong learning. Maintain your curiosity, experiment with new ideas, and seek information. Attend seminars, learn more, and

keep current on financial issues that will affect your future.

4. Make contact with others that share your interests:

Share your experience with others. Participate in forums, meetings, or online groups where like-minded people debate financial independence. Collective wisdom has the potential to be a strong motivator.

5. Reconsider Your Budget:

Examine your finances again. Identify areas for improvement, look for methods to eliminate wasteful costs, and devote greater resources to revenue-generating activities.

6. Create a Portfolio of Passive Income:

Diversify your sources of revenue. Build a solid portfolio that works for you even when you're not working, whether via investments, side projects, or entrepreneurial initiatives.

7. Seek Professional Help:

Consider seeking the advice of financial specialists. Their knowledge and experience can give you specialized insights and tactics geared to your specific financial circumstances.

8. Adopt an Aggressive Retirement Mentality:
Rethink the conventional retirement story. Adopt an active mentality that will position you for a retirement full of plenty, adventure, and the freedom to live life on your own terms.

Remember that your financial journey is a continuous narrative, and every action you do today adds to the chapters of your future. The wisdom of James D. Lynn has prepared the route; now it is up to you to walk it. Start authoring your financial success story now.

Best wishes for a happy future,

[Your Surname]

BONUS

CHECKLIST FOR UNLOCKING FINANCIAL FREEDOM

Congratulations for taking the first step toward financial independence by reading "Get Started: Passive Income, Retirement Adaptability" by James D. Lynn. As an added bonus, here's your own Financial Freedom Checklist to help you get started on the road to financial freedom:

1. Establish Specific Financial Objectives:
Define your short- and long-term financial goals. What goals do you wish to attain on your way to financial independence?

2. Examine Your Present Financial Situation:
Examine your income, spending, obligations, and assets. Understanding your present financial situation is the first step toward making sound financial choices.

3. Determine Your Sources of Passive Income:
Make a list of prospective passive income sources based on your hobbies and available resources. This might include investments, side

projects, or endeavors that are related to your area of expertise.

4. Make an Aggressive Savings Budget:

Create a budget that emphasizes savings. Set aside a sizable amount of your earnings for investments and income-generating possibilities.

5. Investigate New Learning Opportunities:

Commit to lifelong learning. Identify areas where you may improve your personal financial and prospective income-generating abilities and expertise.

6. Get in touch with a Financial Mentor:

Seek advice from someone with financial expertise. A mentor may give useful insights, personal experiences, and specialized counsel.

7. Examine and Improve Your Investments:

Examine your financial portfolio on a regular basis. Investigate new investment alternatives, diversify as needed, and remain current on market developments.

8. Evaluate and Reduce High-Interest Debt:

Pay off high-interest debt first. Create a plan for debt reduction and elimination to free up additional resources for wealth-building activities.

9. Create an Emergency Fund:

Create an emergency fund to handle unanticipated expenditures. Having a financial safety net helps you keep on track even during difficult times.

10. Make Industry Connections:

Participate in industry events, join professional networks, and network with your colleagues. Networking brings you new prospects and keeps you up to date on industry trends.

11. Support Entrepreneurial Ventures:

Investigate business options that match your interests and talents. Entrepreneurship, whether as a side hustle or a full-fledged firm, may be a lucrative source of income.

12. Examine and Modify Your Retirement Plan:

Review your retirement plan on a regular basis. Contributions should be adjusted, retirement objectives should be reassessed, and you should be proactive in maximizing your retirement approach.

13. Monitor and Adjust Your Budget: Constantly monitor and adjust your budget. Identify opportunities for improvement, eliminate wasteful costs, and shift cash to revenue-generating activities.

14. Research Tax techniques: Investigate tax-efficient techniques to enhance your revenue. Keep up to speed on tax regulations and chances to improve your financial situation.

15. Mark Milestones Along the Way: Recognize and appreciate your financial accomplishments. Recognize the milestones you pass on your way to financial independence.

Print this checklist and use it as a road map to help you get closer to financial independence. Every step you take puts you closer to a prosperous and flexible future.

Congratulations on your financial achievement!

www.ingramcontent.com/pod-product-compliance
Lightning Source LLC
Chambersburg PA
CBHW071038290526
45795CB00004B/1213